"Finding ways to stay focused during t
Church's call to prayer, fasting, and alms
In *Lent with Saint Teresa of Calcutta,* Heic ... an effective and
encouraging tool. The daily meditations are filled with warm, personal
storytelling, insightful looks at the life and spirituality of Mother Teresa,
and practical applications for your own life. This devotional book will lead
you to a deeper experience of the Lenten journey and Christ's merciful
love, and leave you readily waiting for the fullness of resurrection joy
when Easter comes."

—COLLEEN MITCHELL, author, *Who Does He Say You Are?*

"This Lent, be instantly drawn into Christ's presence as you experience
daily devotionals inspired by Scripture and the humble, beautiful life of
Mother Teresa. This Lenten devotional, which is intended to be used year
after year, not only invites you on an intimate, daily walk with God, but it
inspires you to become more like St. Teresa and to gain the courage to rely
more upon God as she did throughout her life. Lent is a time for spiritual
growth. *Lent with Saint Teresa of Calcutta* and its glimpse into the heart
of a modern-day saint helps to produce the fertile ground for the seeds of
faith to blossom."

—KATE WICKER, author, *Getting Past Perfect: How to Find
Joy and Grace in the Messiness of Motherhood*

"Heidi Saxton has done it again. How better to draw insight and grace from the lectionary readings than to see them through the eyes and life of St. Teresa. Walk along Mother's footsteps in Calcutta with Heidi and welcome 'Jesus in distressing disguise' into your heart and experience a powerful transformation this Lent."

—BEAR WOZNICK, author, *Deep Adventure* and host of EWTN's "Deep Adventure Radio"

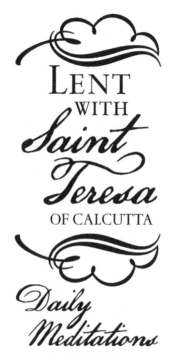

LENT
WITH
Saint
Teresa
OF CALCUTTA

Daily
Meditations

. . . .

Heidi Hess Saxton

servant

AN IMPRINT OF
FRANCISCAN MEDIA
Cincinnati, Ohio

Scripture passages have been taken from *New Revised Standard Version Bible,*
copyright ©1989 by the Division of Christian Education of the National Council
of the Churches of Christ in the U.S.A., and used by permission. All rights reserved.

Cover and book design by Mark Sullivan
Cover image © Corbis | Tim Graham

LIBRARY OF CONGRESS CATALOGING-IN-PUBLICATION DATA
Names: Saxton, Heidi Hess, author.
Title: Lent with Saint Teresa of Calcutta : daily meditations / Heidi Hess
Saxton.
Description: Cincinnati : Servant, 2017. | Includes bibliographical
references.
Identifiers: LCCN 2016042981 | ISBN 9781632531636 (trade paper)
Subjects: LCSH: Lent—Prayers and devotions. | Teresa, Mother, Saint,
1910-1997.
Classification: LCC BX2170.L4 S29 2017 | DDC 242/.34—dc23
LC record available at https://lccn.loc.gov/2016042981

ISBN 978-1-63253-163-6

Contents

Introduction

Lord, teach me to be generous.
Teach me to serve you as you deserve;
  to give and not count the cost;
  to fight and not to heed the wounds;
  to toil and not to seek for rest;
  to labor and not to ask for reward.

> —Prayer of St. Ignatius of Loyola,
> offered daily by the Missionaries of Charity

Just as the physical traits of parents can often be identified in their children and habits and quirks may be passed on through the loving influence of adoptive parents or stepparents, the Missionaries of Charity—in particular, the Sisters—carry on the spiritual charism of their founder. The spirit of Mother Teresa may be found in their passion for the poor, in their tireless and deeply prayerful service, and in their willingness to put their very lives on the line in order to meet the needs of "Jesus in distressing disguise."

The following story about the spiritual daughters of St. Teresa has profound implications for each of us, perhaps especially during Lent when we remember the passion of the Lord; it calls us to consider just how far we are willing to go when the Lord asks us to take up our cross and follow him.

It all began on March 4, 2016. As the Yemeni war for independence ended, evil erupted, showing its truest colors. ISIS was determined to stamp out the last vestiges of a Christian community in Yemen. And so, six months before Mother Teresa was to be canonized, the extremists turned four of her nuns serving at a nursing home in Aden into martyrs, sending them to celebrate with their beloved foundress in eternal glory.

This was not the first time Missionaries of Charity had met with violence since their arrival in Yemen in 1973. Just six years after the order opened the nursing home in Aden in 1992, three Missionaries of Charity Sisters—Sisters Zelia and Aletta of India and Sister Michael from the Philippines—were killed in the Red Sea port of Hodeida, 280 miles northwest of Aden.[1] Since 1998, civil war had devastated the country, already the poorest in the Arab world. "Once a cosmopolitan city home to thriving Hindu and Christian communities," a Vatican Radio correspondent observed, "Aden has gone from one of the world's busiest ports…to a largely lawless backwater. Aden's small Christian population left long ago."[2]

Aden was not safe for them. The Sisters knew this. But they were needed, so they entrusted themselves to God and stayed. Each morning they rose for Mass and Adoration with their chaplain, Father Tom Uzhunnalil, a Salesian missionary from Bangalore who had been staying with them since his own Yemeni parish had been destroyed the previous summer. Then, at about eight o'clock, they set off to tend to the needs of the eighty indigent elderly who resided in the home.

On that Wednesday in March, a group of ISIS gunmen turned up at the nursing home at about 8:30 PM and demanded to be let in, claiming that their mothers were living there. Once inside, they opened fire, killing the gatekeeper instantly.

Hearing the shots, five young Ethiopian workers ran to warn the Sisters and became the first to be caught and executed. The attackers then systematically tied up and shot four Missionaries of Charity Sisters and four others of Ethiopian and Yemeni descent, including a cook who had worked there for fifteen years. The superior, Sister Sally, saw the slaughter and ran to the chapel at the convent to warn Father Tom. But the gunmen had already entered the convent, so Sister Sally ran instead into a refrigerated room in the nursing home and stood behind the door, hidden in plain sight. Sister Sally was the sole survivor; her account was handwritten by two of her Sisters and published by the *National Catholic Register*.[3] According to this account, "At least 3 times they came into the Fridgerator [*sic*] Room. She did not hide but remained standing behind the door—they never saw her. This is miraculous."[4]

Father Tom was abducted. As of this writing, his whereabouts are still unknown.

According to Sister Sally's account, the gunmen left around ten o'clock. Sister Sally went to retrieve the bodies of her Sisters, then to check on the residents inside the home. They were all unharmed.

Hearing of the attack, the cook's son tried and was unable to reach his mother on her cell phone, so he called the police, who arrived at the home at 10:30 AM that morning and discovered the massacre. They persuaded a reluctant Sister Sally to leave, knowing that ISIS would not rest until she, too, was dead. Sister Sally understood this all too well:

Aden is [a] rich city—a port city. Aden wanted to be its own state so they got ISIS in to help them fight against Yemen. So ISIS won for Aden. That was the war last year with all the bombing. They won…but ISIS won't leave. *They* want to take over and exterminate any Christian presence. They did not kill the Sisters in the war because they had no political reason to waste time on them. But now, they are the only Christian presence and ISIS wants to get rid of all Christianity. So they are real martyrs— died because they are Christians. They could have died so many times in the war but God wanted it to be clear they are martyrs for the faith.[5]

The Apostolic Vicariate of Southern Arabia identified the four murdered Sisters as Sister M. Anselm (Binar, India), Sister M. Judith (Kenya), and Sisters M. Margherite and M. Reginette (both from Rwanda). "These are today's martyrs," said Pope Francis. "They are not on the front pages of the newspapers—they are not news. They give their blood for the Church."[6]

When the story of these martyred Christians first began to circulate, rumors spread like wildfire about the fate of the priest—some predicted he would be held for ransom; others asserted that he would be crucified on Good Friday. As of this writing, we know only that the authorities believe him to be alive and are negotiating for his release. For now, his life is hidden in the heart of God (see Colossians 3:3).

The fate of the Sisters, and those who sought to protect them, has no such cruel uncertainty. Though their attackers no doubt intended evil, seeking to destroy the work of the despised Christians, in reality they simply revealed the true nature of these Christians and sent them on to their reward. Having been formed through the influence and teachings of Mother Teresa, the Sisters shone like the brightest gold in their witness. We see that same spiritual courage in the local Christians who died trying to protect the Sisters and in the priest whose first thought was to consume the consecrated Hosts so they would not be desecrated.

This courage showed itself not only in those who died, but in Sister Sally, who tried to warn the priest, who was reluctant to leave because the old people in her care begged her to stay, who felt "so sad because she is alone and did not die with her Sisters."[7] And yet, because her life was miraculously spared, she was able to bear witness to the selflessness that turned an unthinkable act of hatred into a moment of glory.

Thinking about this story in the context of Lent, why not take a few moments to consider: *Had I been there that day, what would I have done?* Although there is no knowing for sure—God tends to give us the strength we need to face such emergencies only in the moment—try to put yourself in the story. Do you see yourself rooted in horror, unable to move? Running to warn or defend the Sisters, as several of their Co-Workers did? Would you have done your best to hide or escape, following the natural impulse of self-preservation? If one of those killed had been a family member or other loved one, would you be tempted to seek revenge or become angry with God for not miraculously saving them all?

Of course, temperament and other personal factors color our first response in crises. And yet, our ability to endure both an emergency and its aftermath depends to a great degree on our ability to turn to God with trust and confidence. The sort of courage the Sisters showed was not the work of a moment, but of a lifetime of prayer and small offerings-up of the annoyances, inconveniences, and trials of daily life. This spirituality is something Mother Teresa understood well and taught her Sisters. Their spirituality is perhaps best captured in the prayer, attributed to John Henry Newman, that they offered in their chapel each morning, which reads in part:

> Dear Lord:
> Help me to spread your fragrance wherever I go.
> Flood my soul with your spirit and life.
> Penetrate and possess my whole being so utterly that all my life may only be a radiance of yours.
>
> …
>
> Let me preach you without preaching, not by words but by my example, by the catching force, the sympathetic influence of what I do, the evident fullness of the love my heart bears to you.
> Amen.[8]

As we contemplate Scripture and the life and teachings of St. Teresa of Calcutta during this Lent, we have a daily inspiration and opportunity to follow her example and that of her community in spreading Christ's fragrance to others. And whatever the future holds—pain or healing, uncertainty or assurance, dismay or delight—we can anticipate with great joy the glory of the Risen Christ at our journey's end.

St. Teresa of Calcutta and your sister martyrs, pray for us.

How to Use This Book

This book is intended to be used from year to year. The penitential season of Lent consists of forty days (not counting Sundays) in which we prepare for Easter, the most resplendent season of the liturgical calendar. Except for Sundays, the daily readings do not change from year to year;[9] and even on Sundays the Gospels focus on the same "core" stories: the Transfiguration, the Samaritan woman at the well, the healing of the blind man by the pool of Beth-zatha, and the raising of Lazarus. These themes of conversion and healing are vital to the Christian life.

Even before her canonization, the life and writings of St. Teresa of Calcutta challenged us to "go deeper," to surrender more fully to Christ's transforming graces, to ponder eternal mysteries and how we are to live them out in our own lives. Since her canonization on September 4, 2016, her writings have become even more important. Inspired by the example of St. Teresa and her Missionaries of Charity—especially the martyred Christians of Yemen who chose to lay down their lives in humble service to accomplish the work God had given them to do—let's take a moment each day to do the same. How? Consider this passage in the Letter to the Colossians:

> So if you have been raised with Christ, seek the things that are above, where Christ is, seated at the right hand of God. Set your minds on things that are above, not on the things that are on earth, for you have died, and your life is hidden with Christ in

God. When Christ who is your life is revealed, then you also will be revealed with him in glory.…

As God's chosen ones, holy and beloved, clothe yourselves with compassion, kindness, humility, meekness, and patience. Bear with one another and…forgive each other; just as the Lord has forgiven you, so you also must forgive. (Colossians 3:1–4, 12–13)

Our daily offering of work and prayer, the intentional giving of ourselves, delights the One who loves us. Each sacrifice, however great or small, presents an opportunity to die to ourselves so that the love of Christ might shine more brightly through us. Together with Christians from all around the world, let us pray that our witness—like that of St. Teresa and her Sisters—might be a transforming force of love.

Week of Ash Wednesday
REMEMBER THAT YOU ARE DUST
(MEMENTO MORI)

Ash Wednesday
THE ROAD OF RECONCILIATION
Joel 2:12–18; Psalm 51:3–4, 5–6, 12–13, 17;
2 Corinthians 5:20—6:2; Matthew 6:1–6, 16–18

We entreat you on behalf of Christ, be reconciled to God. For our sake he made him to be sin who knew no sin, so that in him we might become the righteousness of God.

—2 Corinthians 5:20–21

"Remember that you are dust, and to dust you shall return," intones the priest as he traces a cross-shaped smudge of palm ashes on each forehead. Although Ash Wednesday is not a holy day of obligation, Catholics of every stripe flock to their local parish to participate in the ritual. Some get up early and carry their cross all day, their Catholic identity clearly visible on Facebook and at the water cooler. Others (like me) scuttle by church after work to claim theirs just before the day is done. While this approach protects me from the spiritual pride associated with "bragging rights"… am I truly entering into the spirit of the liturgical season by taking up my cross when it's convenient for my own schedule?

Looking at the life of Mother Teresa, we are reminded over and over again that love does the hard thing, the distasteful thing. Love is not afraid of a little inconvenience or embarrassment. For Lent is not primarily about displaying our ashes; rather, it is about the daily battle to get right with God, about disciplining ourselves in body and soul through this annual pilgrimage of penitence. With our prayers, fasting, and almsgiving, we respond to the invitation to *memento mori* ("remember death"), putting into proper perspective our need to die a little each day so that Christ might live within us.

One of the best ways to do this is to receive not just ashes, but absolution. In the spring of 2014, Pope Francis reminded the crowd at one of his Wednesday audiences of the power of the sacrament of reconciliation:

> Everyone say to himself: "When was the last time I went to confession?" And if it has been a long time, don't lose another day! Go, the priest will be good. And Jesus [will be] there, and Jesus is better than the priests—Jesus receives you. He will receive you with so much love! Be courageous, and go to confession.[10]

This "road of reconciliation," following in the footsteps of the sinless One who took on our shame and guilt so that we need no longer carry it, is the pathway every saint has walked and every aspiring saint must follow. When our hearts are clean and whole through the graces of the sacrament, remembering death becomes not a morbid preoccupation, but a sign of hope—for ourselves and for all those who look at us and see the likeness of the Savior. As Mother Teresa said,

> I'm very happy if you can see Jesus in me, because I can see Jesus in you. But holiness is not just for a few people. It's for everyone, including you.... Holiness is the greatest gift that God can give us because for that reason He created us.[11]

A Moment to Reflect

- Look in the mirror and study the cross on your forehead. What kind of cross were you given to carry? Is it big and bold? Barely visible? What is God saying to you about what he wants for you this Lent?
- Is it time for you to go to confession? The Church teaches that we need to go to confession at least once a year, or whenever we are conscious of having committed serious sin (see *CCC* 2042). Don't worry if it's been a while—God is waiting to meet you there. Don't settle for ashes alone when you can receive absolution and a fresh start!

A Moment to Pray

Lord Jesus, as I start my Lenten journey, I confess that I still have far to go on the "road of reconciliation." Give me the courage I need to follow you, as St. Teresa did, even when the road is hard. Holy Spirit, work in me so that one day I too might be a saint! St. Teresa of Calcutta, pray for us!

Thursday after Ash Wednesday
SAD SAINT, BAD SAINT
Deuteronomy 30:15–20; Psalm 1:1–2, 3–4, 6; Luke 9:22–25

Happy are those
  who do not follow the advice of the wicked,
or take the path that sinners tread,
  or sit in the seat of scoffers;
but their delight is in the law of the Lord,
  and on his law they meditate day and night. They are like trees
  planted by streams of water, which yield their fruit in its
season,
  and their leaves do not wither. In all that they do, they prosper.
                                        —Psalm 1:1–3

Mother Teresa tended to broken souls and bodies at every age and from every walk of life. From the Indian children at Nirmala Shishu Bhavan to the elderly in Nirmal Hriday (Home for the Dying), the Missionaries of Charity still uplift and comfort the truly desperate and helpless. They live and work right in the struggle, sinking their roots deep where they have been planted out of love for God. Often there is no miracle cure, not even a deathbed conversion for all the love and prayer they pour into their work. Yet they remain faithful to the work they believe God calls them to do.

I often think of Mother Teresa when I grow discouraged about parenting Chris and Sarah, biological siblings my husband Craig and I adopted in

2005. As parents we watch over them with great hope as they struggle in their never-ending battle of nurture vs. nature. To be honest, there are days when I think God brought these kids into our lives as much to save us as to help them. As I face the challenges of motherhood, my flaws are glaringly apparent. Efforts to *will* our children into wholeness have at times been the source of tremendous anxiety and pain for all concerned.

One day I confessed this to Father John, a gentle and holy priest from Nigeria, who listened patiently as I poured out my concerns. Then he encouraged my husband and me to let him offer the children some spiritual direction and to go sit with them in front of the Blessed Sacrament so that we could experience God's healing presence as a family. Finally, he urged us to be patient. "Just remind them every day that you love them, that you believe in them," he concluded. "There is great power in the love of a parent. They do not need things to be happy.... They need to know your heart."

"Get your praise on," another friend advised me. She meant that I should sing my praises to God, which is always a good thing to do. But in my heart, I heard: "Your children need to hear your praise. So lift up your heart, find your joy...and go get your praise on!"

This "call to joy" is a frequent theme in the writings of Mother Teresa, a relentless summons to peace and joy based not on our current circumstances, but on a simple recognition of who we are in Christ.

> Mother Teresa loved to remind her Sisters of the call to joy, recalling the words of St. Francis de Sales, "A sad saint is a bad saint."

Mother Teresa observed, "Saint Teresa of Avila worried about her sisters only when she saw them lose their joy. Joy is a source of power for us."[12]

And so today you must decide. Are you going to scan the horizon, looking for the dark clouds ahead and worrying about the future? Or are you going to sink your roots deep into the Living Water and trust God to send a fruitful harvest of peace, joy, and love?

A Moment to Reflect

- Was there a moment you wish you could do over, when you had an opportunity to choose joy and didn't? Tell God about that. Thank God for being your joy and strength.
- Do you want to be a "bad saint" or a "glad saint"? What situations do you anticipate encountering, for which you will need an extra shot of grace in order to respond with joy? Why not ask God for those graces now?

A Moment to Pray

God, you are my strength and my song. You are the reason for my joy. Fill me with your Holy Spirit, and drive away the forces of discouragement and despair. Jesus, I trust in you! St. Teresa of Calcutta, pray for us!

Friday after Ash Wednesday
BAKED BEAN MOMENTS
Isaiah 58:1–9*a*; Psalm 51:3–4, 5–6*ab*, 18–19; Matthew 9:14–15

Is not this the fast that I choose:
   to loose the bonds of injustice,
   to undo the thongs of the yoke,
to let the oppressed go free,
   and to break every yoke?
Is it not to share your bread with the hungry,
   and bring the homeless poor into your house…?

—Isaiah 58:6–7

The human tendency to steer our actions according to our personal pref-erences can be difficult to overcome—yet it is a key part of learning the virtue of detachment. So, on Fridays in Lent, when Catholic moms across the country, mindful of Lenten rules of fasting and abstinence, wrack their brains to come up with a meatless supper solution, I know just what to fix: baked bean casserole.

It's a bit hypocritical, I suppose. I used to hate this recipe of my mother's with the burning fire of a thousand suns…and now I'm visiting the same culinary discipline on my own kids.

Why?

My attachment to this particular card in my recipe file goes back at least forty years, to a twelve-hour hunger strike I declared at the age of six, when my parents decided I was going to eat a whole plateful. Money was tight, and no child of *theirs* was going to turn up her nose at good, home-cooked food.

Nibbling a slice of bread and butter, I eyed those beans on my plate and refused to take a bite.

They insisted.

I dug in my heels. I sat in front of that plate of congealed beans until bedtime, only to find a bowl of them at my place, cold, the following morning for breakfast. "You better eat them," my father warned. "Or you'll get them tonight while we all eat hot dogs!"

That threat finally convinced me to gag the things down. Though I was not yet Catholic, that day I learned a bit about the importance of detachment and obedience as a way to overcome self-will.

And do you know what? Over time, my taste buds grew up and I discovered at some point that those beans weren't half bad. Today, in fact, I'm not sure I hate them nearly enough to get a single soul out of purgatory by eating them.

My daughter does, though. And so…the circle of life.

I thought of this story when I read of an encounter with Mother Teresa and a group of reporters who wanted to take her picture. While food never seemed to be a difficult area of detachment for her—she and her Sisters ate with thanks whatever God provided—it turns out she had a distaste for the limelight and kept reporters at arm's length in much the same way I treated that molasses-and-onion-riddled bean mash. She, too, came to see the glory in enduring a little suffering for a higher purpose.

> Despite her iconic status as an advocate for the poor of the world, Mother Teresa hated having her picture taken. One of her sisters recalled: "She would tell journalists that for every photo

they snapped she asked Jesus to please take a suffering soul out of purgatory. 'For me it is more difficult than bathing a leper,' she said."[13]

Mother Teresa was likely the most photographed Catholic religious of all time. Just think of how many souls have her to thank for her offering up her personal aversion out of love for God and dedication to the people she'd been called to serve.

Most of us, if we think about it, have a personal aversion to something. We do our utmost to avoid having to deal with it—be it something consumed or worn, or someone with whom we just don't get along. Wednesday's ashes call us to remember another kind of death—a death to self, for the sake of a more important goal.

On Fridays in Lent, we are called to give up something, to make a personal sacrifice of some kind out of love for God. And while bellying up to "endless shrimp" is technically abstaining from meat...is it really the kind of thing that can truly be called a "sacrifice"? What would represent a true sacrifice for you, something that can only be done (or refused) out of love?

A Moment to Reflect

- Is it a real sacrifice for you to give up meat on Fridays in Lent? What habit or practice do you think God is asking you to relinquish (or take up) in order to grow closer to him?
- Is there some area of your life in which you need God's help to grow stronger or more disciplined? Post a note on your refrigerator, bathroom mirror, or car visor—a prayer of thanksgiving to God, for giving you the strength you need to succeed.

A Moment to Pray

Lord Jesus, you did not teach your disciples to ask God to supply their needs a month or even a week at a time. Rather, you taught us to say, "Give us this day our daily bread." Just for today, Lord, give me strength to say no to self and yes to you. St. Teresa of Calcutta, pray for us!

Saturday after Ash Wednesday
IS YOUR LAMP SHINING?
Isaiah 58:9b–14; Psalm 86:1–2, 3–4, 5–6; Luke 5:27–32

If you remove the yoke from among you,
    the pointing of the finger, the speaking of evil, if you offer
your food to the hungry
    and satisfy the needs of the afflicted, then your light shall rise
in the darkness
    and your gloom be like the noonday.

—Isaiah 58:9b–10

Think about the last time you encountered a homeless person or a person begging for change on the side of the road—perhaps with a hand-lettered sign bearing the humiliating details of his or her life.

"Got to feed my kids."

"Will work for food."

"Army vet. Hungry. Please help."

When was the last time you passed by one of these individuals and took a moment to look him or her full in the face? To smile and engage the person in the kind of social banter you'd exchange at the grocery store or in line at the post office?

It can be hard, I know. But life is short, and lives are precious; these are the "least of these" Jesus wants us to love in his name.

When did a human cry for help become…embarrassing? I say this having been brought up short on more than one occasion by my daughter, who challenges me: "Hey, Mom. That man looks hungry. Can we give him this apple?"

Why, yes, honey. Yes, we can.

Mother Teresa understood that poverty has a dehumanizing effect on the soul, the kind that robs a person of his very dignity. She taught her Sisters to work against that particular wrong, not just with a handout of food but with their very presence.

This saintly nun recounted the story of meeting an Aboriginal man in Australia who lived in squalor. Entering his house, Mother Teresa noticed a beautiful lamp that had obviously not been used for a long time. When she asked whether he lit the lamp, the man replied, "For whom? No one ever comes to my house. I spend days without seeing a human face. I have no need to light the lamp." Mother asked if he would light the lamp if her Sisters came to visit him every evening, and the man agreed. She writes:

> The sisters made it their habit to visit him every evening. The old man began to light the lamp for them and to keep it clean. He began to keep his house clean, too. He lived for two more years….[Visiting him] was a very small thing, but in that dark loneliness a light was lit and continued to shine.[14]

Most of us at some point were afraid of the dark; as children we would beg our parents to leave on the hall light or a night-light because it kept the darkness at bay. As we grew older, we learned to live with the darkness, and the fear went away for most of us. Even so, as the shadows grow long it becomes all too easy to overlook what is right before our eyes.

Don't forget to light your lamp. Don't forget to speak, to lend a hand when you can. Above all, don't forget what a kindness it can be to ask someone to leave his lamp burning, to give him confidence that he won't always be alone.

A Moment to Reflect

- What did you do today to lighten the darkness for or assuage the loneliness of another soul? How did someone do that for you?
- If you can, go to your local parish and pay a visit to the tabernacle, where the lamp is always burning brightly to signify the presence of the Eucharistic Lord. Every day, Jesus is there waiting for you.

A Moment to Pray

How often, Lord Jesus, did you feel alone when you were here on earth? How often did you long for companionship, for kindness? Help me, Lord, the next time I see a lonely soul, to look in his eyes and see you there. St. Teresa of Calcutta, pray for us!

First Week of Lent
TURNING TOWARD GOD

First Sunday of Lent
WHAT IS YOUR DAILY BREAD?
Year A: Genesis 2:7–9, 3:1–7; Psalm 51:3–4, 5–6, 12–13, 17;
Romans 5:12–19; Matthew 4:1–11
Year B: Genesis 9:8–15; Psalm 25:4–5, 6–7, 8–9;
1 Peter 3:18–22; Mark 1:12–15
Year C: Deuteronomy 26:4–10; Psalm 91:1–2, 10–11, 12–13, 14–15;
Romans 10:8–13; Luke 4:1–13

Then Jesus was led up by the Spirit into the wilderness to be tempted by the devil. He fasted forty days and forty nights, and afterwards he was famished. The tempter came and said to him, "If you are the Son of God, command these stones to become loaves of bread." But he answered, "It is written,

'One does not live by bread alone,
but by every word that comes from the mouth of God.'"

—Matthew 4:1–4

In today's Gospel about the temptation of Christ, we can see that when tempting the New Adam, the devil appeals first to the desire of the flesh, knowing Christ is hungry: "Command these stones to become loaves of bread" (Matthew 4:3).

Now, on the face of it, this temptation seems like such a small thing. What would have been the harm, really, if Jesus had turned a few stones into bread? Surely God wouldn't have wanted his Son to be hungry. Jesus later fed thousands of people with his miracle of bread and fish; was this so very different?

It was. In resisting the devil, the Lord gained victory over mankind's first deadly sin—when the serpent enticed our first parents to doubt God's love and justice by taking and eating the forbidden fruit: "Did God say, 'You shall not eat from any tree in the garden'?" (Genesis 3:1). Just a bite of fruit…no big deal, really. Except that, in disregarding God's words and refusing to stay within the boundaries he had set up for their own protection, they brought about the fall of the human race.

Facing the devil in that moment, Jesus understood what was at stake. The One who was to become our "daily bread" threw himself on the mercy, love, and justice of his Father (see Matthew 4:4).

The temptation was real…and so was the victory.

This Gospel narrative teaches us a great deal about the nature of the temptations we face each day. So often the devil hits with a subtle suggestion at the very point we are most vulnerable. Just a small concession, for a really good reason—what could it possibly matter? Just one small compromise. One tiny step off the path. One little "white lie." One unkind word, or a wink and grin at someone else's moral lapse. It's not a really *big* sin, just a venial offense, not even worth mentioning in confession…or is it? Listen to the words of Mother Teresa:

If we deliberately allow venial sin to become a daily bread, a moral anemia, the soul becomes weak all around, the spiritual life begins to crumble and fall apart. God preserve us from any deliberate sin, no matter how small it may be. Nothing is small when it comes to going against God.[15]

In any battle, the enemy does not show his power until he is sure he has his opponent surrounded and ensnared. A terrorist does not announce his deadly intention, but blends into the crowd in order to surprise his targets. Likewise, evil's favorite cover is an insipid form of social tolerance that justifies even the deadliest of sins.

It is up to us, then, to make sure we take our fill of the right "daily bread," feeding on the very life of Christ in the sacraments and in the Word of God; these will give us strength to resist the subtle whisperings of the enemy that "small" sins couldn't possibly matter to God.

A Moment to Reflect
- Can you think of a moment when you were being tempted? What made you particularly vulnerable? What might you do in the future to better resist that temptation?
- Ask God to make you particularly vigilant, able to see temptations for what they are and to recognize how "small" sins can cause great damage to the soul.

A Moment to Pray
Holy Spirit, sweep through the spaces of my heart and remove any traces of pride; help me to resist temptation and to listen to your voice whenever I, like Adam and Eve, am tempted to give in to the serpent's snare. St. Teresa of Calcutta, pray for us!

Monday of the First Week of Lent
You Did It to Me

Leviticus 19:1–2, 11–18; Psalm 19:8, 9, 10, 15; Matthew 25:31–46

Truly I tell you, just as you did it to one of the least of these who are members of my family, you did it to me.

—Matthew 25:40

A prolific British journalist with an acerbic wit, Malcolm Muggeridge (1903–1990) was perhaps best known for his outspoken and sometimes irreverent political commentary. He also introduced the world to Mother Teresa, first in a 1967 interview for the BBC and later in his documentary and book, both called *Something Beautiful for God,* about his encounter with her.

Muggeridge, who for most of his life claimed to be an agnostic, traveled all over the world as a foreign correspondent and became a celebrated television personality on the BBC. His encounter later in life with the work of Mother Teresa and her Sisters among the poor and utterly powerless at Nirmal Hriday had a life-changing effect that ultimately led him into the Catholic Church. The tenderness of the nuns, a reflection of ministering to the Lord they loved in his "distressing disguise," was a powerful witness to the agnostic journalist.

In the book, Muggeridge recounts a harrowing story from his time in Calcutta in which he takes a man who has been accidentally injured to the hospital for treatment.

It was a scene of inconceivable confusion and horror.… It was too much; I made off, back to my comfortable flat and a stiff whisky and soda…. I ran away and stayed away; Mother Teresa moved in and stayed. That was the difference.[16]

It must have been a bit embarrassing for this sophisticated world traveler who had never backed away from a challenge to be shown up by a diminutive nun. It is no easy thing to be confronted with our own softness, our own sense of entitlement and privilege, when it comes to facing the harsh realities of how many other people live.

Perhaps that is why Mother Teresa would so frequently brush aside offers of money in order to urge the benefactor to give more: to give of himself or herself. [17] Though those who want to help the Missionaries of Charity are never turned away, it is not essential to go across the world in order to respond to the needs of the poor and vulnerable. Those who are ready and willing to follow in the footsteps of this saint and her Sisters can begin by responding to the needs of their neighbors by practicing the corporal and spiritual works of mercy with greater intentionality, as much for their own sakes as for those of their neighbors (*CCC* 2447). These works of mercy, spiritual and corporal, are:

- *Feed the hungry; give drink to the thirsty.* In giving from our abundance, we practice temperance.
- *Counsel the doubtful.* In pointing those experiencing moments of doubt not just to an intellectual awareness of Jesus, but toward spending time in his presence, we build up our own faith.
- *Shelter the homeless.* In welcoming the stranger, we practice diligent kindness.
- *Instruct the ignorant.* In sharing our faith, we continue to build up our own understanding of what the Church teaches and why.

- *Clothe the naked.* In protecting another's dignity, we practice modesty and chastity.
- *Admonish the sinner.* In recognizing that love that is not truthful is not love—and truth that is not loving is not truth, we learn to balance mercy and justice.
- *Forgive injuries and bear wrongs patiently.* Endeavoring to treat others with this kind of gentle courtesy helps us recall how much we have been forgiven.
- *Visit the sick and imprisoned.* In committing ourselves to be constrained as they are, even for a short time, we practice humility.
- *Comfort the sorrowful.* In offering the gift of silent presence, which often speaks more loudly than words, we practice fortitude.
- *Bury the dead.* In bearing another's grief, we acknowledge the need for community and practice true charity, knowing it cannot be reciprocated.
- *Pray for the living and the dead.* As we intercede for the needs of others, we live out in a very practical way the reality of the communion of the saints and the bonds that even death cannot sever.
- *Give alms to the poor.* As the *Catechism* points out, "Giving alms to the poor is one of the chief witnesses to fraternal charity: it is also a work of justice pleasing to God" (*CCC* 2447).

A Moment to Reflect
- Was there a particular moment today when you had an opportunity to "love the least of these"? What happened, and how did you respond?

- Which of the corporal and spiritual works of mercy do you find most challenging? When you are tempted simply to do nothing, what might be a better response?

A Moment to Pray

Lord, we are on the earth for such a short time— just long enough to do the tasks you have entrusted to us and to grow in holiness so that one day we might be ready for the joys of heaven. Lord Jesus, what do you want me to do for you today? St. Teresa of Calcutta, pray for us!

Tuesday of the First Week of Lent

FIRST THOUGHTS OF THE DAY

Isaiah 55:10–11; Psalm 34:4–5, 6–7, 16–17, 18–19; Matthew 6:7–15

> When you are praying, do not heap up empty phrases…for your Father knows what you need before you ask him.
>
> —Matthew 6:7–8

What was the first thought you had upon waking this morning? Were your first coherent thoughts colored by negativity, anxiety, worry, or strife? Did you leap out of bed and start chiding yourself about the million things you needed to do before breakfast? Mother Teresa asks:

> Does your mind and your heart go to Jesus as soon as you get up in the morning? This is prayer, that you turn your mind and heart to God. In your times of difficulties, in sorrows, in sufferings, in temptations, and in all things, where did your mind and heart turn first of all? How did you pray? Did you take the trouble to turn to Jesus and pray, or did you seek consolations?[18]

No doubt that first sip of your favorite morning brew beckons to you. But while the kettle boils or the coffee percolates, take a moment to reorient yourself, to acknowledge your debt and dependence upon the One who set the universe in space, who kept you breathing through the night, who set his angels to guard your house while you and your family slept. Prayer is a debt of love, to be sure—and yet that simple gesture of reminding ourselves that we are not truly the center of the universe, holding it all together, can have a liberating effect.

Good morning, Lord. Thank you for watching over us last night…

If you're anything like me, it might take a little effort to see the "good" in morning. I've never been a "morning person," and as with most Catholic moms, my life is replete with late nights, family issues, work challenges, and physical challenges that could leave a person scrambling to find something for which to be thankful.

Yet over the years I've learned that my day always goes better when I stop and thank God anyway. Starting from a position of thanks and trust in Divine Providence makes it easier to face whatever is in store. Besides, I need a regular reminder that I cannot control or dictate every circumstance of my life—some things are just beyond my control. And when those unexpected challenges arise, turning spontaneously to God to share both thanks and concerns helps me get through the day, from breakfast to bedtime.

In his book *Introduction to the Devout Life,* St. Francis de Sales writes of the importance of lifting the soul up to God in prayer each day:

> Prayer opens the understanding to the brightness of Divine Light, and the will to the warmth of Heavenly Love—nothing can so effectually purify the mind from its many ignorances, or the will from its perverse affections. It is as a healing water which causes the roots of our good desires to send forth fresh shoots, which washes away the soul's imperfections, and allays the thirst of passion.[19]

How often do you experience healing waters, the "warmth of Heavenly Love"? Does your day begin with the siren song of the snooze alarm or a hungry toddler and throttle on relentlessly until you tumble, exhausted, into bed? If that happens to you more often than you'd like to admit, how can you take advantage of this Lenten season to begin a new and healthier approach to prayer?

Some who are just beginning the discipline of morning prayer find it helpful to remember the acronym ACTS (Adoration, Contrition, Thanksgiving, and Supplication), which provides a simple way to begin each day:

- I worship you, God, because _____.
- I'm sorry, God, because _____.
- Thank you, God, for _____.
- Help me, God, to _____.

A Moment to Reflect

- What's the first thing you remember about the events of your morning? Did you feel tired or cheerful, anxious or at peace? As the day progressed, was there a good time for you to pause and breathe a prayer of thanks to God?
- The "ACTS" prayer can be a useful tool for staying in touch with God throughout the day—even just a sentence or two. As you go through your day, think about moments when you might turn to God in adoration, contrition, thanksgiving, and supplication. How do these prayers change your outlook?

A Moment to Pray

Holy Spirit, you are the sign of God's love in the world, guiding me and speaking to me through the circumstances of my life. Raise my mind to worship, caution me when I go astray, prompt me when I need to intercede for another. I thank you for remaining with me always. St. Teresa of Calcutta, pray for us!

Wednesday of the First Week of Lent
GIFTS OF GRACE
Jonah 3:1‒10; Psalm 51:3‒4, 12‒13, 18‒19; Luke 11:29‒32

Create in me a clean heart, O God,
　　and put a new and right spirit within me. Do not cast me away
from your presence,
　　and do not take your holy spirit from me. Restore to me the
joy of your salvation,
　　and sustain in me a willing spirit.

—Psalm 51:10–12

Most of us have wished at one time or another that life had a "do-over" button (or an "unsend" button for e-mail). This was true even of King David, the second king of Israel, whom God called "a man after my heart" (Acts 13:22). As today's penitential psalm, attributed to King David, reminds us, even spiritual giants like David sinned spectacularly at times (see 2 Samuel 11—12).[20]

It's difficult to say, really, what David might have regretted most about his dalliance with Bathsheba, which was replete with arrogance, lust, and deception. Was it the dereliction of duty that caused him to be idly strolling alone on the rooftop of the palace, gazing lasciviously over the palace wall (2 Samuel 11:2–3)? Was it the abuse of power that led him to pressure Bathsheba to submit to his desire (11:4–5)? Murdering her husband Uriah in a desperate attempt to cover their adultery, and then marrying the widow in unseemly haste (11:14–27)? Or was it simply the knowledge that his actions had fooled no one, least of all God (12:1–15)?

And yet, what is most remarkable about this story is that, despite the child's death, we still get a glimpse of God's lavish grace. Upon learning that the child Bathsheba bore him had died, he said:

> "While the child was still alive, I fasted and wept; for I said 'Who knows? The Lord may be gracious to me, and the child may live.' But now he is dead.… Can I bring him back again?…" Then David consoled his wife Bathsheba,…and she bore a son, and he named him Solomon. (2 Samuel 12:22–24)

In other words, King Solomon, the wisest man who had ever lived (see 1 Kings 4:30) and the future architect of the first great Temple, was a gift of unmitigated grace in the face of overwhelming guilt.

"Create in me a clean heart, O God," David pleads, remorseful beyond measure. It is this urge to be reconciled to God, this firm resolve to mend the breach that has torn the relationship asunder, that fills the heart that is truly penitent. In those moments of remorse, we do not merely seek relief from the guilt (or "fire insurance" from the prospect of eternal damnation); instead, we hope, like David, to be once more truly united to the heart of God.

I have no doubt that at times Mother Teresa felt this urgency to be reconciled with her Beloved, though we do not know what forms her weaknesses and sins may have taken. We do know that she struggled through times of great desolation, though these spiritual "dry spells" are often a sign of divine favor, an opportunity for growth. Mother Teresa certainly understood the need to keep short accounts with God, to keep her heart clean and open to receive him:

A clean heart can see God, can speak to God, and can see the love of God in others. When you have a clean heart it means you are open and honest with God, you are not hiding anything from Him, and this lets Him take what He wants from you.[21]

Through the Church, we have the ability to receive a visitation of grace, especially through the sacrament of reconciliation, if we are prepared to be honest with God and make a good confession. We can approach the sacrament at the lowest point of our lives, with sins as serious as those of King David, and receive absolution. We can also open our hearts to receive these graces simply because we want to experience union with God, as did St. Teresa. Either way, we can be assured of one thing: out of the generous heart of God spring gifts of grace based not on what we deserve, but on how much he loves.

A Moment to Reflect
- Can you think of a time today when God was generous with you? When God looks at you, what do you think he sees?
- Do you anticipate encountering anyone who needs to experience God's unmitigated grace? What can you do to help that person receive what is needed?

A Moment to Pray
Almighty God, whose ways are often so mysterious, whose mercies are new every morning, go before me and show me how to share the story of your abundant grace in my life. Let me be a sign of hope to all those I encounter. St. Teresa of Calcutta, pray for us!

Thursday of the First Week of Lent
NINE LEVELS OF CHARITY
Commentary on Esther C:12, 14–16, 23–25; Psalm 138:1–8; Matthew 7:7–12

> Is there anyone among you who, if your child asks for bread, will
> give a stone? Or if the child asks for a fish, will give a snake?…
> How much more will your Father in heaven give good things to
> those who ask him!
>
> —Matthew 7:9–11

Does it matter what motivates us to give to others, or the way we offer our
gift? Are some kinds of generosity more laudable than others? Jesus taught
about the meaning of true generosity in the parable of the widow's mite
(see Luke 21:1–4). In the eyes of the Lord, the poor widow's small but
heartfelt offering was of infinitely greater value than the larger gifts of the
rich who share only what they can easily spare. When the purpose of our
gift becomes more about making ourselves feel noble than about easing
the suffering of another human being, our "bread" turns into stone; our
"fishes" into snakes, as those we intend to help experience the shame of
becoming an object of charity.

The twelfth-century Jewish philosopher, astronomer, and prolific Torah
scholar Moses Maimonides taught that there are eight levels or forms of
giving, each taking into consideration not only the intention of the giver,
but the long- and short-term effect on the recipient:

> The first and lowest degree is to give, but with reluctance or
> regret. This is the gift of the hand, but not the heart.

The second degree is to give cheerfully, but not in proportion to the distress of the sufferer.

The third degree is to give cheerfully and in proportion to the suffering, but not until the gift is solicited.

The fourth degree is to give cheerfully, proportionally, and even unsolicited, but to put it in the poor man's hand, thereby shaming him.

The fifth degree is to give charity in such a way that the distressed may receive the bounty, and know their benefactor without being known by him.

The sixth degree is to know the objects of one's bounty, but to remain unknown to them.

The seventh degree…[is] to bestow charity in such a way that the benefactor may not know the relieved person, nor they the name of the benefactor.

The eighth degree, and the most meritorious of all, is to anticipate charity by preventing poverty. That is, to assist the reduced fellow man…by teaching him a trade, or by putting him in the way of business so that he may earn an honest livelihood and not be forced to the dreadful alternative of holding out his hand for charity. [22]

In her address upon receiving the Nobel Peace Prize in 1979, Mother Teresa spoke of what seems to me to be a ninth level of giving, arguably even higher than these eight envisioned by Maimonides. At Mother Teresa's level, the act of giving is a source of joy for giver and receiver alike, based entirely on love:

Some time ago in Calcutta we had great difficulty in getting sugar, and I don't know how the word got around to the children, and a little boy of four years old, a Hindu boy, went home and told his parents: I will not eat sugar for three days, I will give my sugar to Mother Teresa for her children. After three days his father and mother brought him to our home. I had never met them before, and this little one could scarcely pronounce my name, but he knew exactly what he had come to do. He knew that he wanted to share his love.[23]

A Moment to Reflect

- Think about the last time you made a donation of money, time, or goods. Which level of giving did you experience? How might you have reached a higher level?
- Have you or someone close to you ever been on the receiving end of charitable giving? How did you feel about it—and did the way you received the gift make a difference?

A Moment to Pray

Father God, you have been so generous with me. Thank you for all your many gifts. [*Name some of them here.*] Help me, like the boy with the sugar, to be a source of joy to those you give me a chance to help. St. Teresa of Calcutta, pray for us!

Friday of the First Week of Lent
GOD LOVES U-TURNS
Ezekiel 18:21–28; Psalm 130:1–8; Matthew 5:20–26

So when you are offering your gift at the altar, if you remember
that your brother or sister has something against you, leave your
gift there before the altar and go; first be reconciled to your
brother or sister, and then come and offer your gift.

—Matthew 5:23–24

In the book *Reaching Out in Love,* Mother Teresa recalls a time in the early
years of the foundation of her schools for poor children when someone
donated sixteen beautiful saris. She decided to present them to the girls
at the children's home Nirmala Shishu Bhavan on the next day, their feast
day.

But overnight thieves broke in, and the saris were among the stolen
things. Mother Teresa gathered the girls and urged them to ask God to
return the stolen saris…and just as the ceremony was about to begin, the
police called to notify her that their property had been recovered.

Joyfully delivering the news to the children, Mother Teresa added,
"Everything starts with prayer. God always answers our prayer though we
sometimes do not get what we asked for. God knows what is best for us."[24]

We do not know what happened to those who were caught stealing,
whether they were punished for the theft or even whether Mother Teresa
later met with those souls who were so lost that they would stoop to
stealing even clothing to improve their lot. However, it is very likely that
the experience made a deep impression upon the girls, who followed

Mother Teresa's counsel to pray for God's intervention and had their beautiful saris returned to them. Being reminded that the Heavenly Father cares for their every need must have been an important milestone in the spiritual lives of those fatherless girls.

By encouraging the girls to focus not on their loss, but on divine providence, Mother Teresa gently guided them away from the temptation to harbor unforgiveness or resentment toward those who had stolen their precious saris. Because of her wisdom, even if the dresses had not been returned to them, the girls would not have been robbed of the joy of that day.

Today's Gospel reminds us of a similar truth: that God is pleased with the offering of those whose hearts are fully open to him, not harboring the toxic burden of resentment or unforgiveness. Only the heart that is fully open and trusting can hope to receive his blessing.

This is why Jesus taught that reconciliation is a prerequisite for grace; this spiritual "U-turn" is as much for our own benefit as it is for the person who has offended us. The healing balm of forgiveness clears a path for God to work on both sides of the divide.

A Moment to Reflect

- Did someone cross your path today—or cross your mind, without a physical encounter—who has done something to hurt you or someone you love? Is God calling you to "leave your gift at the altar" and make peace?
- What is the benefit to you of seeking to reconcile any broken relationship, even if the other person has not asked for forgiveness, and even if you no longer have contact with this person?

A Moment to Pray

Lord Jesus, when I think of how far you went to bring me back into relationship with God, even giving up your own life on the cross, I realize that the wounds that have been inflicted on me are nothing compared to yours. Help me to walk with small but even steps the gentle way of forgiveness. St. Teresa of Calcutta, pray for us!

Saturday of the First Week of Lent
FINDING THE WAY OF HAPPINESS
Deuteronomy 26:16–19; Psalm 119:1–2, 4–5, 7–8; Matthew 5:43–48

Happy are those whose way is blameless,
  who walk in the law of the Lord.…
O that my ways may be steadfast
  in keeping your statutes!…
I will praise you with an upright heart,
  when I learn your righteous ordinances. I will observe your
statutes;
  do not utterly forsake me.

—Psalm 119:1, 5, 7–8

Do you want to be happy? Today's psalm gives us the recipe for finding happiness in this life, a recipe that can be summed up in one of Mother Teresa's favorite words: *obedience.* Through obedience we are able to overcome temptation, to live in a way that pleases God, and to bring light to a dark and dying world.

Of course, this particular spiritual habit has fallen out of favor in contemporary culture, but the *Catechism* reminds us that "the duty of obedience requires all to give due honor to authority and to treat those who are charged to exercise it with respect, and…with gratitude and good-will" (*CCC* 1900).

St. Teresa spoke often to her Sisters about obeying God, not just from a sense of begrudging duty, but out of wholehearted love. "Be faithful in the little things, for in them lies our strength," she said. [25] Obedience, she believed, is at the heart of a strong vocation.

> My vocation is grounded in belonging to Jesus, and in the firm conviction that nothing will separate me from the love of Christ. The work we do is nothing more than a means of transforming our love for Christ into something concrete. I didn't have to find Jesus. Jesus found me and chose me. A strong vocation is based on being possessed by Christ. It means loving him with undivided attention and faithfulness through the freedom of poverty and total self-surrender through obedience. [26]

As we complete this first full week of Lent, in which we focused on how to overcome temptation and fight the dark impulses both within and around us, it's good to reorient ourselves toward our ultimate goal, which is to attain heaven by following Jesus as closely as possible. We fix our eyes on the task we have been given, ask for pardon for those areas in which we have faltered or failed, and ask for the grace to begin again.

To be perfectly frank, it is unlikely that we will be called upon to bathe a leper or run an orphanage or hold the hand of a dying soul picked up from the streets. And yet, we too have been charged with fulfilling our vocations not simply from a sense of duty, but out of wholehearted love for God.

And so, "I will praise you with an upright heart..." (Psalm 119:7):

I will praise you, God, when I am so bone-weary I can barely get myself, let alone the squirming, hungry noisemakers you have entrusted to me, ready for Mass.

I will praise you, God, when the people I am trying to help in your name are ornery, unappreciative, or grumpy. Help me to see in them, as St. Teresa did, "Jesus in distressing disguise."

I will praise you, God, when you give me an unexpected taste of poverty or humility. Help me to trust you to provide exactly what I need, exactly when I need it.

I will praise you, God, when the circumstances of my life tempt me to take shortcuts or compromise what I know to be right, true, and good. I will praise you, too, when I blow it and need to experience the healing balm of your mercy.

I will praise you, God, that every day you give me a fresh opportunity to embrace my vocation and to touch the lives of others with beauty, goodness, and truth. Help me to walk that way without faltering. Above all, teach me the joy of obedience.

A Moment to Reflect

- Was there a particular time today when you struggled to embrace your vocation or when obedience was a difficult choice to make?
- Remember that God is faithful, even when we are not. If you have a particular area of struggle, Jesus is waiting to give you the strength you need in the sacraments of penance and Eucharist. Don't be afraid!

A Moment to Pray

Lord Jesus, thank you for your love that sustains me, even in the darkest moments of my life. Thank you that you came to earth to walk the way of obedience, so that I can follow you not just out of duty but out of love. Strengthen me to continue this journey in the coming week. St. Teresa of Calcutta, pray for us!

Second Week of Lent
Transforming Acts of Love

Second Sunday of Lent
A Transforming Encounter
Year A: Genesis 12:1–4a; Psalm 33:4–5, 18–19, 20, 22;
2 Timothy 1:8–10; Matthew 17:1–9
Year B: Genesis 22:1–2, 9a, 10–13, 15–18; Psalm 116:10, 15, 16–17, 18–19;
Romans 8:31b–34; Mark 9:2–10
Year C: Genesis 15:5–12, 17–18; Psalm 27:1, 7–8a, 8b–9, 13–14;
Philippians 3:17—4:1; Luke 9:28b–36

Six days later, Jesus…was transfigured before them, and his face shone like the sun, and his clothes became dazzling white. Suddenly there appeared to them Moses and Elijah, talking with him.

—Matthew 17:1–3

Although the Sunday Gospel readings are on a three-year cycle, the Lenten Sunday readings always include the same four stories that are crucial to our understanding of the salvation story. These narratives and their associated evangelical and spiritual themes are the Transfiguration of Jesus (transforming acts of love), Jesus speaking to the Samaritan woman (called to conversion), Jesus healing the man born blind (be healed), and Jesus raising Lazarus from the dead (raised to new life).

This week we take up the first of these, the moment when the eyes of Jesus's disciples were opened and they truly encountered the divinity of their Master, who stood in the company of Moses (revealing Jesus as the fulfillment of the Law) and Elijah (revealing Jesus as the perfect fulfillment of the words of the prophets).

We meditate on the transforming power of scripture, coming to understand—as did the disciples—that this revelation of Christ's divinity is not the end of our journey, but the beginning. Jesus did not take Peter up on his offer to build a place for them to stay and revel in the glory of the Transfiguration. And when God the Father broke into the conversation and declared Jesus "my Son, the Beloved" (17:5), Jesus roused the disciples, assuring them that they had nothing to fear. The Lord's revelation of himself to his disciples set them on a lifelong journey of personal transformation and of witnessing to the truth of what they had been shown. Similarly, when we truly encounter Christ—in the scriptures or in the sacraments—it sets us off on a journey of transformation and witness that takes a lifetime to complete.

Lent is a special time of preparation—of watering those seeds that were planted within us at baptism and weeding our gardens to give those seeds ample room to grow—in order to experience a joyful encounter with the Risen Christ at Easter. The nature of each person's encounter is unique, according to our need. For St. Paul, encounter with Christ meant being struck blind on the road to Damascus (Acts 9:3–9); for the woman caught in adultery, it involved a gentle admonishment to "go and sin no more" (John 8:1–11). But most of these encounters have one thing in common: "Ask, and it will be given you; search, and you will find; knock, and the door will be opened for you," Jesus tells us (Matthew 7:7).

Mother Teresa's life-changing encounter took place when she was in her mid-thirties through a sudden and unmistakable "call within a call." She had already stepped outside her comfort zone by leaving her home in Albania in order to become a professed Loreto nun in Calcutta, educating upper-class Indian girls at St. Mary's School during the 1930s and 1940s. Then, on September 10, 1946, her life took an even more dramatic turn while she was on a train ride from Calcutta to Darjeeling, where she was to make a retreat. On that train Mother Teresa had an encounter with Jesus that dramatically changed the course of her life and led her to found the Missionaries of Charity; the order was officially instituted on October 7, 1950.

This part of St. Teresa's story has important implications for anyone who has felt the restless tug of the Holy Spirit precipitating a kind of spiritual "midlife crisis." Maybe you've just been going through the motions when it comes to attending Mass or loving your spouse or kids or performing in some other area of your life. Or maybe you sense that God is asking something new of you, such as becoming a catechist or taking a class or changing jobs or welcoming another child into your home.

It can be a bit terrifying. You know there are no guarantees, but Jesus says the same thing to you that he said to Peter: "Get up and do not be afraid" (Matthew 17:7).

My "call within a call" happened in the summer of 1993. After nearly thirty years as an evangelical Christian, including four years in missionary training, I found myself traveling across eastern Europe as the leader of a short-term missions group. Our group comprised twenty-seven college students: half were charismatic Christians from Poland, and the other half were non-charismatic Americans (Baptists, Quakers, and a smattering of nondenominational Christians). By the end of the summer, exhausted and spiritually depleted from the stress of the extraordinary adventure, I took refuge in the last place I ever expected to find God—a little Catholic mission parish in South Pasadena, California. I sneaked into weekly Mass for almost six months before I finally worked up the nerve to enroll in RCIA.

And the rest, as they say, is history. Five years later, I met my husband. Five years after that, we adopted Chris and Sarah. Following God's call transformed me from single-lady missionary to wife, mother, and Catholic editor. I didn't plan it that way—couldn't have imagined it, in fact. I just kept saying yes and taking another step forward, trusting that God could see ahead even when I could not.

A Moment to Reflect
- Is there an area of your life God is asking you to change or relinquish so he can transform you? What do you think is holding you back?
- What is one thing you could do to take a tiny step forward to the next yes?

A Moment to Pray
Jesus, shine your divine light into my heart. Reveal any place that is dark or hard or in need of your healing light. Give me courage not to hold

back, to step out in faith wherever you want me to go, to do whatever you want me to do. Transform me, beginning today. St. Teresa of Calcutta, pray for us!

Monday of the Second Week of Lent
A MERCIFUL ME
Daniel 9:4b–10; Psalm 79:8, 9, 11, 13; Luke 6:36–38

Be merciful, just as your Father is merciful.

—Luke 6:36

In September 1978, Mother Teresa was invited to address those in attendance at the Freiburg *Katholikentag*, a lay-organized religious festival of
German-speaking Catholics from Germany, Switzerland, and Austria.
The German bishops had also invited then-Archbishop Karol Wojtyla,
but God had other plans. Pope Paul VI died just a few weeks before the
event, and the archbishop emerged from the conclave as Pope John Paul
II. Perhaps providentially, the theme of the German festival was "God's
Call: Our Way." Mother Teresa rose and shared with those in attendance
about the power of the Eucharist to strengthen her and her Sisters to do
the work God had called them to do—not their way, but God's:

> To live out such a calling every Missionary of Charity must have
> a life focused on the Eucharist. We see Christ in the Eucharist
> under the appearance of bread, while we see him in the poor
> under the distressing disguise of poverty…. The sisters care for
> forty-nine thousand lepers. They are among the most unwanted,
> unloved, and neglected people. The other day one of our sisters
> was washing a leper covered in sores. A Muslim holy man was
> present, standing close to her. He said, "All these years I have
> believed that Jesus Christ is a prophet. Today I believe that Jesus

Christ is God since he has been able to give such joy to this sister, so that she can do her work with so much love."[27]

Mother Teresa's simple testimony about the transforming mercy of God and the power of the Eucharist to strengthen us to do the impossible speaks to us as we reflect upon today's Gospel. When Jesus says, "Be merciful, just as your Father is merciful," he is speaking of extending mercy not only to our friends and those we love, but also to the "other," the stranger and even the enemy, transforming them into brothers and sisters. "If you love those who love you," Jesus asks, "what credit is that to you? For even sinners love those who love them" (Luke 6:32).

As Mother Teresa's story reminds us, the miracle of the Eucharist is not that it transforms the stranger or enemy so that we might like them better or that they might become more like us. The miracle is that it transforms us! As we open our hearts to receive the Lord—Body and Blood, Soul and Divinity—we become better able to love, by God's grace, even the most unlikely and unlovable, until they are irresistibly drawn to that heavenly love themselves. As Mother Teresa said, "What we say does not matter, only what God says to souls through us."[28]

One day shortly after our children arrived, I heard the doorbell ring and opened the door to find an elderly Jehovah's Witness, tracts in hand, standing on my doorstep. I'd had a total of twenty minutes of sleep the previous night and hadn't cracked open a Bible in weeks. But something prompted me to open the door and let the old man in. His dark hands caressed the worn cover of his Bible, and he talked with me about how much he loved reading it for hours every day. I told him that I envied him, and he looked surprised.

"Really?"

"Yes," I said. "There was a time in my life when I spent hours reading the Bible and other good books, as a theology student. But now I have small children, and I'm lucky to have five minutes to myself. Do you know how I spend time with God now, what gets me through?"

He shook his head.

"I sit with Jesus in the chapel and ask his mother to watch over me and my kids. And then I go on with my life, knowing that they are both watching over me. I don't know if I could get through this time of my life if I didn't have that source of strength."

This was not what he had expected. When he heard "theology student," he had started rifling through the pages of his Bible, preparing himself to engage in a hearty exchange of theological posturing and out-of-context proof-texting.

Instead, the next thing he heard was the confession of an overwhelmed mom. I saw his eyes soften, and he got up to go. I don't know what he made of our encounter. I do know that, in a situation in which I once would have relished an energetic exchange of ideas with the goal of stumping my opponent, I watched a brother in Christ, a soul God loves, go in peace. I hoped that he saw a merciful me.

A Moment to Reflect

- What opportunities did you have today to encounter people who don't believe the same things you do? How would you characterize those encounters? Would they have known you are a disciple of Christ?

- When was the last time you visited Jesus during the week in

Adoration? Why not make a short visit to a nearby chapel and receive a little more mercy to take with you through the day?

A Moment to Pray

Merciful Father, you are Love itself. Fill me with your spirit so that I might love more perfectly, more mercifully, more completely. Let others look at me and see Jesus. St. Teresa of Calcutta, pray for us!

Tuesday of the Second Week of Lent

CALLING ALL FATHERS

Isaiah 1:10, 16–20; Psalm 50:8–9, 16bc–17, 21, 23; Matthew 23:1–12

And call no one your father on earth, for you have one Father—
the one in heaven.

—Matthew 23:9

Shortly after our wedding, my husband and I decided that I would quit work for a time so that we could start a family and I could go back to school to get a graduate degree in theology, which would come in handy for a Catholic publishing professional. I enrolled in a program for lay students at a seminary about an hour from my home, and for the next year I drove in two or three times a week to take classes.

I was mildly surprised one day in the seminary cafeteria when one of my priest-teachers plunked his lunch tray down next to mine. After a few minutes of casual conversation, he asked me if it were true that I was writing an exposé about life at the seminary.

I thought he was kidding me. I chuckled nervously.

He wasn't kidding. On the contrary, he looked at me earnestly and inquired further, "Heidi, do you want to be a priest? Is that why you're here?"

Incredulous, I set down my fork. "Father, let me put your mind at rest about that. Most days I can barely handle one vocation. Why on *earth* would I want a second one?"

He relaxed visibly and picked up his fork, and we had a pleasant meal together.

Our kids arrived not long after that awkward lunch conversation took place, and the program that should have taken me two years stretched out into nearly seven. More than once I thought about that conversation and laughed. Truer words had never been spoken than when I told my professor I had all I could handle with the one vocation. I knew there were women who believed passionately that women should be priests. I just didn't happen to be one of them…any more than I believed my classmates had it in them to switch places with me. God had called me, all right. But no one would ever call me "Father."

In his Letter to the Romans, the apostle Paul writes, "For as in one body we have many members, and not all the members have the same function, so we, who are many, are one body in Christ, and individually we are members of one another. We have gifts that differ according to the grace given to us…" (12:4–6). St. Teresa understood this complementarity of giftedness, recognizing that the work of her Sisters had its limits and that there was a time when they needed the ministrations of a priest. She believed with all her heart that priests had an indispensable role in bringing a soul to God. At the same 1978 event in Freiburg described in yesterday's meditation, Mother Teresa made an urgent appeal to the young men who were present:

> Our sisters work in many countries around the world. They work with society's outcasts. One day the sisters came across a man who had locked himself away from everyone. He lived in a tightly shut room. The sisters came in, washed his clothes, cleaned his room, and bathed him. All the while he did not say a word. Two days later he told the sisters: "You have brought God into my life. Bring me also a priest." The sisters brought him a

priest, and he made his confession for the first time in sixty years. The next morning he died.

Oh, how great is the vocation of the priesthood! God had come into that man's life, but he needed a priest to come into contact with God's mercy and forgiveness. He needed the ministry of a priest to take away his sins, to wash his sins away in the precious blood of Christ.

You, young men, whom Jesus has called, whom Jesus has chosen for his own, consider the call to be that bridge that can link souls to God.[29]

A Moment to Reflect

- Can you remember a time when you wrestled with feelings of envy or regret concerning your vocation, or wished that you could use your God-given gifts in a different way? Do you know someone who is discerning a religious vocation who could use your prayers right now?
- As you go about your day, thank God for the opportunities you have to use your gifts within your vocation, right where you are. Do you see opportunities to do more? Talk to God about what he is calling you to do!

A Moment to Pray

Heavenly Father, all over the world there are men and women who need courage to follow the path to the religious life that you are calling them to take. Give me grace to pray for them when they need those prayers most. St. Teresa of Calcutta, pray for us!

Wednesday of the Second Week of Lent
THE PERFECT MOTHER'S HEART
Jeremiah 18:18–20; Psalm 31:5–6, 14, 15–16; Matthew 20:17–28

It will not be so among you; but whoever wishes to be great among you must be your servant, and whoever wishes to be first among you must be your slave.

—Matthew 20:26–28

As any parent of a special-needs kid will tell you, we spend a great deal of time advocating for our children at their schools in order to give them the best chance of success. We reach out regularly to teachers, even several times each week, to make sure the lines of communication stay open. We know how quickly our children can get off track and are painfully aware that the teachers are already overburdened with crowded classrooms, minimal resources, and troubled students whose erratic behavior and performance create real classroom management problems. Most days, we just hope that our kids aren't in the thick of it.

And so I have to smile a little when reading today's Gospel, in which the mother of the sons of Zebedee (James and John) approaches Jesus and asks him to give her sons special treatment.

Jesus must have regarded her with great compassion. She was not, after all, omniscient; she had no way of knowing how the story would end: "Then two bandits were crucified with him, one on his right and one on his left" (Matthew 27:38). Yes, in the end there would be men on his right and left…but not the way she had meant. Had she foreseen the reality, she would surely have turned and fled, dragging her sons with her.

49

The other disciples, indignant, chastised the "mama's boys." For his part, Jesus responded by redefining what it means to be a leader. Greatness, he said to the disciples, is not about who stands in the spotlight, but about who buses the tables.

Still, you have to appreciate where Mrs. Zebedee was coming from. A mother's love is a fierce and tireless force of nature. That's not altogether a bad thing—it gives mothers energy to nurture children around the clock. It can also wreak tremendous devastation if we mothers do not learn to respect the boundaries of human dignity and allow our children to exercise free will as appropriate to their stage of development.

By contrast, think of the role the Blessed Mother played in the life of her Son. Her love was poured out on Jesus from the moment she understood that she was to be a mother, when she offered her yes to God sincerely and without reservation. While she appears at times throughout the Gospel narrative, Mary does not come across as forceful or "pushy," nor does she try to hold on to Jesus—even when it means that the words of Simeon would be fulfilled: "This child is destined for the falling and the rising of many in Israel, and to be a sign that will be opposed so that the inner thoughts of many will be revealed—and a sword will pierce your own soul too" (Luke 2:34–35).

Mother Teresa had a great devotion to the Blessed Mother, whom she regarded as a sure way to the heart of Jesus:

> Immaculate Heart of Mary, our Queen and Mother, be more and more our way to Jesus, the light of Jesus, and the life of Jesus in each one of us. In return for this gift, let us be more and more a cause of joy to one another, the way of peace to one another and the living of love of Jesus for one another.[30]

Let us try to imitate her gentle way, continually drawing all those who come near ever closer to Mary's beloved Son. Let us be true children of Mary, each doing our part to transform the world in love.

A Moment to Reflect

- As you read today's meditation, did you think of a time when the actions of your child or some other loved one embarrassed you—or caused you to live vicariously through their achievements? How did it affect your relationship?
- When you think of Mary, what event in the life of Christ do you most associate with her maternal care for him? How do you most often experience that care?

A Moment to Pray

Blessed Mother, you were a guiding light in the life of Christ, encouraging him to fulfill his mission without pride or envy or fear. Pray for me, that my love for those in my care will guide them well, without compulsion or the need to control. St. Teresa of Calcutta, pray for us!

Thursday of the Second Week of Lent
A CHASM OF FAITH
Jeremiah 17:5–10; Psalm 1:1–2, 3, 4, 6; Luke 16:19–31

Besides all this, between you and us a great chasm has been fixed,
so that those who might want to pass from here to you cannot do
so, and no one can cross from there to us.

—Luke 16:26

Just after I turned eighteen, I got a job as a server at a steak restaurant several miles from home. One evening only a few days into the job, I was driving home from work when my car slid on a patch of black ice and skidded downhill into oncoming traffic. I woke up in the hospital a week later, sure that God had spared my life and determined to find out why.

One of the greatest challenges I faced at that time was deciding whether to get married to the young man I was dating or to go for missionary training, something I believed God was calling me to do. The young man did not share the same faith as my family, so to those closest to me the right course of action was clear: break things off and go serve God. For me, it was agony to feel compelled to choose God over my heart. My burden of grief and resentment isolated me from God for a long time; I felt as though I stood, separated from him, on the far side of some dark chasm of faith. But gradually, over time, I discovered that God had not made unreasonable demands on me and then abandoned me as it seemed; rather, he was working to transform me—ultimately leading me into the Catholic Church.

When I first read of the "dark nights" of Mother Teresa, I mistakenly interpreted her experience as similar to my own distancing from God. Only gradually as I began to learn more about the Catholic faith did I understand that her sense of isolation or "darkness," as she called it, came from a very different source. Hers was not a distance or chasm of her own making; rather, it was the consequence of a life lived in intimate union with God.

In his book *I Loved Jesus in the Night,* Paul Murray records a line from Mother Teresa's December 3, 1947, letter to Calcutta Archbishop Ferdinand Périer, SJ: "If I ever become a saint—I will surely be one of 'darkness.'" Murray explains:

> This darkness was not…an experience of depression or despair. Rather it was the shadow cast in her soul by the overwhelming light of God's presence: God utterly present and yet utterly hidden. His intimate, purifying love experienced as a devastating absence and even, on occasion, as a complete abandonment.[31]

In an article in the *New York Times*, "A Saint's Dark Night," Father James Martin further interprets Mother Teresa's experience:

> In time, with the aid of the priest who acted as her spiritual director, Mother Teresa concluded that these painful experiences could help her identify not only with the abandonment that Jesus Christ felt during the crucifixion, but also with the abandonment that the poor faced daily. In this way she hoped to enter, in her words, the "dark holes" of the lives of the people with whom she worked. Paradoxically, then, Mother Teresa's

doubt may have contributed to the efficacy of one of the more notable faith-based initiatives of the last century.[32]

One of the important lessons to take from Mother Teresa's life is the importance of finding competent support when one encounters a time of darkness, whether circumstantial, emanating from some inner struggle, or stemming from chronic depression or anger or guilt. Being accountable to a priest or spiritual director who can help discern the source of the darkness prevents us from being caught in the prison of our own design. Some who suffer may need medical attention or counseling; others find relief in the sacraments—particularly the sacrament of reconciliation. However, if the time comes when we experience true desolation, we can shoulder that burden knowing that—no matter what—we can, like St. Teresa, still choose to be joyful in God.

A Moment to Reflect

- Was there a moment when you, like St. Teresa, chose to embrace joy even as you were going through a time of doubt or other darkness?
- What are the areas and moments of life in which you are most susceptible to emotional downswings? What are some ways you can choose faith over feelings?

A Moment to Pray

Mother Mary, you must have known great sadness in your lifetime, and at times the circumstances must have been overwhelming. Pray for me when I feel that the darkness is threatening to overtake me. Stay with me until the morning light. St. Teresa of Calcutta, pray for us!

Friday of the Second Week of Lent
WHEN OUR LOVE FAILS

Genesis 37:3‾4, 12‾13a, 17b‾28a; Psalm 105:16‾17, 18‾19, 20‾21;
Matthew 21:33‾43, 45‾46

Finally he sent his son to them, saying, "They will respect my
son." But when the tenants saw the son, they said to themselves,
"This is the heir; come, let us kill him and get his inheritance."
So they seized him, threw him out of the vineyard, and killed
him.

—Matthew 21:37–39

As I read about the life and work of Mother Teresa, it did not surprise
me to discover that she and her Sisters often encountered small miracles
in their work: the infant revived through St. Teresa's prayer, the hard-
drinking agnostic who became a Catholic through her influence. What
I found unsettling were the times when she extended herself for a living
soul…and there was no happy ending to the story.

As the mother of two teenagers, I was particularly affected by the story
of one young drug addict Mother Teresa and her companions encountered in London, a young, long-haired man they found sitting with several
others on the side of the street. Mother Teresa writes:

And I said to him: "Why are you here? You shouldn't be here. You
should be home with your parents." The young man shook his
head. "Mother, so often I tried to go home. My mother doesn't

want me. Each time I go home, she pushes me out because she can't bear my long hair."

I gave him some soup and sandwiches and we passed on. On our way back, we found him lying flat on the ground. He had overdosed himself with drugs....

I couldn't help but reflect: here is a child hungry for home, and his mother has no time for him. This is great poverty. This is where you and I must make this a better world.[33]

When it comes to addiction, there is often no "better world" in store for those who are unwilling or unable to break free from whatever has them bound. Simply welcoming the young man home would not have solved the problem. It's entirely possible that his mother was trying to protect younger siblings from the influence of his addiction, or that she had other serious reasons for turning him away that had nothing to do with the length of his hair. It's also very likely that his mother's heart broke when she discovered her son had died on the street, and that she grieved for the fact that the time for reconciliation and healing was past.

Today's Gospel speaks of the real consequences of estrangement and the long-reaching effects of relational breakdown. In the parable of the wicked tenants, a landowner plants a vineyard, leases it to tenants, and leaves the country, sending his servants back at harvest time to collect the produce. Clearly the tenants have no loyalty to this absentee landlord; they abuse his representatives and even kill the landowner's own son to get his inheritance. Such a sense of antagonism and entitlement is hard to imagine. And yet, when we remember that we are all merely stewards of everything God has given us…is the reaction of the tenants in this parable really that far-fetched?

Let's consider this on a more personal level. How often do we find ourselves resenting giving God his due? Do we give generously and joyfully, according to true justice rather than self-interest? How often do we damage others with our words or actions out of annoyance, stress, or anger?

How often are we the wicked tenants?

How often does our love fail?

A Moment to Reflect

- Is there someone from whom you are currently estranged? Is God asking you to lay the groundwork for reconciliation before it is too late?
- When we offer the Our Father, we ask God to "forgive us our trespasses, as we forgive those who trespass against us." As you go about your day, ask yourself: *Do I ask God for greater mercy than I am willing to give?*

A Moment to Pray

Divine Master, I want to be a faithful steward, to please you in all I say and do. Help me to be generous in love and mercy and to be fair with those who most need my help. St. Teresa of Calcutta, pray for us!

Saturday of the Second Week of Lent
THE SATISFIED SOUL
Micah 7:14–15, 18–20; Psalm 103:1–2, 3–4, 9–10, 11–12; Luke 15:1–3, 11–32

Bless the Lord, O my soul,

and do not forget all his benefits— who forgives all your iniquity,

who heals all your diseases, who redeems your life from the Pit,

who crowns you with steadfast love and mercy…

—Psalm 103:2–4

Right after high school, I auditioned for a part in a community theater production of *Godspell.* I had coveted the part of Mary Magdalene; it was my chance to break out of my shell and don that feather boa with all the pent-up exuberance of a young woman who, thanks to a conservative upbringing, had spent her high-school years in "granny skirts." A friend of mine, someone with stronger pipes and stage presence, got the part, and I was crushed. I consoled myself by buying the sound track and singing myself hoarse in the car. "Oh, bless the Lord, my soul," indeed.

Just a few weeks after the audition, I was belting out a few bars on my way home from work when my car accident occurred. Hospitalized for over a month, I got out just in time to catch the show's final performance. The director, a kind man who had kept in touch since the accident, called me up on stage and gave me flowers. It was a golden moment for me, standing there in the limelight on crutches and clutching my bouquet.

I belonged. The director's simple gesture was a transforming act of love.

Now, my devastation after losing that part had been a "first-world problem": I had a family who loved me, a home, and food and medical care when I needed it. Not getting a part in a play shouldn't have been that big a deal. But the diva in me had been craving proof that I was special, that I was worthwhile, that I belonged. At that time in my life, finding acceptance and belonging was as important to me as the air I breathed.

Decades later, as a mom, I recognize this same quest for a sense of significance in my own teenagers and their peers. So did Mother Teresa. When she gave her Nobel Peace Prize address in 1979, she talked about a Western variety of poverty:

> I found the poverty of the West so much more difficult to remove. When I pick up a person from the street, hungry, I give him a plate of rice, a piece of bread, I have satisfied, I have removed that hunger. But a person who is shut out, that feels unwanted, unloved, terrified, the person that has been thrown out from society—that poverty is so hurtful, and so much, that I find it very difficult.[34]

This kind of poverty is not found exclusively among the underprivileged. In fact, some would argue that it is more prevalent in two-income households in which children are left to their own devices for prolonged periods without their parents' finding ways to maintain that personal connection. Mother Teresa urged parents to address this void in family life:

> When [children] come home there is no one in the family there to receive them. Our children depend on us for everything— their health, their nutrition, their security, their coming to know

and love God. For all this they come to us with trust, hope, and expectation.... Love the poor, but first of all love the members of your own family.[35]

The wise saint reminds us that the most important gifts we can offer our children cannot be purchased. This transformational sense of connection and significance, this inner satisfaction of the soul, must be cultivated through relationship—relationship with family and friends and, above all, relationship with God. As today's psalm reminds us, when we remember his goodness to us, then our souls can be truly satisfied.

A Moment to Reflect
- Which of God's blessings or "benefits" have you received today for which you are you most thankful? How have you experienced God's love for you?
- What is one thing you can do tomorrow to satisfy the soul of someone who is lonely or looking for significance?

A Moment to Pray
St. Teresa, you spent your lifetime raising up souls who had fallen into poverty and isolation and drawing them to the light of God. Pray for me, that I might perform this service for someone out of love for Christ. St. Teresa of Calcutta, pray for us!

Third Week of Lent
CALLED TO CONVERSION

Third Sunday of Lent
THIRSTING FOR SOULS
Year A: Exodus 17:3–7; Psalm 95:1–2, 6–7, 8–9;
Romans 5:1–2, 5–8; John 4:5–42
Year B: Exodus 20:1–17; Psalm 19:8, 9, 10, 11;
1 Corinthians 1:22–25; John 2:13–25
Year C: Exodus 3:1–8*a*, 13–15; Psalm 103:1–2, 3–4, 6–7, 8, 11;
1 Corinthians 10:1–6, 10–12; Luke 13:1–9

Jesus answered her, "If you knew the gift of God, and who it is
that is saying to you, 'Give me a drink,' you would have asked
him, and he would have given you living water."

—John 4:10

In today's Gospel, Jesus again reveals his divine nature—this time to a
Samaritan woman, member of a religious culture so estranged from that
of the Jews that it would have horrified Jesus's followers to see him even
speak with her, let alone accept a cup of water from her hand. Perhaps this

is why the Lord sends his followers to go buy food, then reaches out to this woman who is so lost in her own shame that she has come to draw water at a time when no other decent woman would be present. He focuses not on the potential scandal of their meeting, but on quenching the awful thirst within her.

Reading over this Gospel passage, I am struck by the similarities between the Lord's actions toward the "untouchable" woman in this narrative and those of St. Teresa toward the "untouchables" (also called *Dalits)* in the hovels and gutters of Calcutta, where she tended even those who had been abandoned by their own families with a mother's loving care. In his article "The Scandal of Mother Teresa," Catholic journalist Filip Mazurczak observes that the *Dalits* had often been targets of violence and segregation. Upper-caste Indians would pass them by, but caste made no difference to Mother Teresa. [36]

Mother Teresa expressed her maternity most often by attending to the immediate physical needs of all those she encountered. She and her Sisters did not reserve a higher level of care for Christian families, nor is there any evidence that she pressured Hindus and Muslims to convert. In an August 26, 2013, article in *The Hindu,* Navin Chawla (a Hindu biographer of Mother Teresa) remembers her as someone who intentionally left conversions to God.

> Though staunchly and devoutly Catholic, she reached out to people of all denominations irrespective of their faith, or even the lack of it.… While she lifted the abandoned baby off a street full of prowling dogs for the sanctuary of her Shishu Bhawan, she would never convert her, because that child would probably

be adopted into a nice Hindu household.… In my 23 years of close association with her, she never once whispered that perhaps her religion was superior to mine, or through it lay a shorter route to the Divine.[37]

Nevertheless, Jesus was at the very center of every thought and action of Mother Teresa and her Sisters, who regarded everything they did as an opportunity to satiate the loving thirst of Christ for souls by bringing them closer to him. In *Mother Teresa: Come Be My Light,* Father Brian Kolodiejchuk writes that this focus of Mother Teresa's intensified after she heard the 1993 Lenten message of Pope John Paul II in which he called the faithful to listen to the voice of Jesus, "who, tired and thirsty, says to the Samaritan woman at Jacob's well: 'Give me a drink' (John 4:7). Look upon Jesus nailed to the Cross, dying, and listen to his faint voice: 'I thirst' (John 19:28). Today, Christ repeats his request and relieves the torments of his Passion in the poorest of our brothers and sisters."[38]

"After the pope's Lenten message," writes Father Kolodiejchuk, "Jesus's thirst again became a recurrent theme in Mother Teresa's letters and instructions to her followers. She was sharing what she had been living. All her labors, her sufferings and her joys were only the means to that end."[39]

A Moment to Reflect

- Did you have any opportunities today to satiate the thirst of Christ? What does this look like for you in your vocation?
- What lessons do you draw from the life of Mother Teresa with regard to respecting the dignity of others and the difference between evangelization and proselytizing?

A Moment to Pray

Holy Spirit, I know that it is ultimately your job—not mine—to convert souls. Help me to be faithful in planting seeds of faith in the hearts of those I meet and leaving the harvest to you alone. St. Teresa of Calcutta, pray for us!

Monday of the Third Week of Lent

ST. JOSEPH, MAN OF INTEGRITY

2 Kings 5:1–15a; Psalm 42:2–3; 43:3–4; Luke 4:24–30

And he said, "Truly I tell you, no prophet is accepted in the prophet's hometown."

—Luke 4:24

Every year on March 19 (unless that date falls on a Sunday), Catholic families celebrate the feast of St. Joseph, which represents a bright spot in what is otherwise a penitential season. Italian families and parishes in particular celebrate in a big way with "St. Joseph's Table," a celebration of good food and family, replete with special pastries and seafood-based dishes liberally sprinkled with bread crumbs (representing the sawdust from the carpenter's workbench).

Mother Teresa had a special devotion to St. Joseph as the patron of families and workers and prominently displayed his picture at her order's motherhouse. She turned to him often when there was a need, as we discover in *Thirsting for God*:

> We trust in the power of the name of Jesus and also in the intercessory power of St. Joseph. When we first started our society, there were times when we had nothing. We kept a picture of St. Joseph which we turned face down during those times we were in great need. This reminded us to ask for his intercession. When something came in, we turned it right side up.[40]

The truth is that Scripture doesn't tell us a great deal about Mary's husband. There are a few casual references, such as this one, which precedes today's Gospel:

> All spoke well of [Jesus] and were amazed at the gracious words that came from his mouth. They said, "Is not this Joseph's son?" He said to them, "Doubtless you will quote to me this proverb, 'Doctor, cure yourself!' And you will say, 'Do here also in your hometown the things that we have heard you did at Capernaum'" (Luke 4:22–23).

We don't know for sure how old St. Joseph was, or whether he was a widower, when he was betrothed to Mary; we also do not know how old Jesus was when St. Joseph died. This patron saint of families makes his final appearance in the Gospel narratives when he and Mary find the twelve-year-old Jesus in the Temple (see Luke 2:46).

We can surmise what kind of man St. Joseph was based on what is said about him in the beginning of Matthew's Gospel, which shows us the "righteous" man who refused to shame his pregnant fiancée (1:19), the humble man who obeyed God in everything (1:20–25), and the self-assured man who protected the Holy Family (2:13–15). Mother Teresa had this to say about him:

> When [St. Joseph] saw Our Lady was pregnant—that she was going to have a baby—immediately he was hurt. But he loved Our Lady. Deep down in his heart he loved her and he knew in his mind, "If I go to the priest and tell, immediately they will stone her." He did not know that Our Lady had conceived by the power of the Spirit, but he knew that if he told she would be

stoned....[41] So what did he decide? "I will not tell. I will leave her and go away and people will blame me."[42] This is love.[43]

We also know something else very important: God chose St. Joseph above every other man to guide his own Son to manhood. As with Mary, much of what Joseph did on behalf of Jesus went unseen and unsung. This speaks of a special kind of integrity, the kind that acts according to what is right, even when no one but God is watching. It is this steadfast, humble spirit that makes St. Joseph one of the most beloved of all Catholic saints.

A Moment to Reflect

- What did you do (or are you going to do) to celebrate St. Joseph's feast day? It's not too late...how about sprinkling a few crushed-up cookies (to resemble sawdust from the carpenter's bench) on your favorite ice cream?
- When you think about St. Joseph, what characteristic of his do you most admire or would you most like to imitate?

A Moment to Pray

St. Joseph, thank you for watching over my family and for your prayers in times of trouble. Please pray for me, that I be unafraid to do extraordinary things for God just as you did. St. Teresa of Calcutta, pray for us!

Tuesday of the Third Week of Lent
SEVENTY-SEVEN TIMES?
Daniel 3:25, 34–43; Psalm 25:4bc–5ab, 6, 7bc, 8–9; Matthew 18:21–35

Then Peter came and said to him, "Lord, if another member of the church sins against me, how often should I forgive? As many as seven times?" Jesus said to him, "Not seven times, but, I tell you, seventy-seven times."

—Matthew 18:21–22

In January 1973, Mother Teresa was interviewed by Ralph Rolls on a BBC program entitled *Belief and Life*. Referring to the conflict in Northern Ireland, Rolls asked her to talk about what Christians needed to do to bring peace to the region. Her advice was readily reduced into one simple word: *forgiveness*.

"I have seen…several families that I have visited where someone was murdered or someone died violently," she said. "There is no prejudice in these families. I have seen that these families have forgiven and don't hold any grudges against the ones who killed their sons. I think this is the first step."[44] She went on to say that it isn't absolutely necessary to be a Christian to forgive. "Every human being comes from the hand of God, and we all know something of God's love for us. Whatever our religion, we know that if we really want to love, we must learn to forgive before anything else."[45]

The kind of forgiveness of which Mother Teresa spoke was not the grudging verbal exchange that parents sometimes prompt their children to make:

"Tommy, tell Susie you're sorry for hitting her."

"SOR-ry." (Insert eye roll and a stealthy pinch when Mom is no longer looking.)

The adult version of this formula produces the kind of grudging acknowledgment of wrong that Peter is so quick to quantify and seek to limit in today's Gospel.

No, the "seventy-seven times" kind of forgiveness goes much deeper, transforming not just individuals but entire countries desperately in need of peace. As Mother Teresa moved from one refugee camp to the next, she found that these places "were like one big Calvary where Christ was crucified once more.... Unless there is forgiveness there will be no peace. And forgiveness begins with personal attitudes."[46]

At the heart of "seventy-seven times" forgiveness is surrender—an acknowledgment of our own pitiful inability to comprehend the Infinite and the urgent necessity of relinquishing any personal "rights" to the inscrutable will of God.

It was this kind of forgiveness that prompted the confession of Job: "Naked I came from my mother's womb, and naked I shall return there; the Lord gave, and the Lord has taken away; blessed be the name of the Lord" (Job 1:21). It was this kind of forgiveness that enabled the Samaritan woman to let go of her past regrets and wrongdoing in order to quench her own desperate thirst with the Living Water—and then run and tell the world about the gift she'd been given. And it was this kind of forgiveness that enabled Mary to endure as she stood beneath the cross, watching her beloved Son die a criminal's death.

"Seventy-seven times" forgiveness acknowledges that I do not see the whole story, that God does not love me more than he loves those with whom I am in conflict. It is absolute surrender to Love, an extravagant kind of grace, an undeserved forgiveness that holds out a hand that may be refused. It does not swell up with pride for having undertaken the remarkable. Rather, it makes itself so small that when the other person looks, there is only Jesus to see.

Such grace-powered forgiveness requires blind trust that does not waver even in the face of danger. When Mother Teresa sent her Sisters to Gaza at the height of a conflict, they discovered that the walls of the parish house in which they were to live were stained with the blood of a priest who had been murdered there just the previous day. "The Sisters held their breath as the Superior in an act of faith answered, 'We stay.'"[47]

Because "seventy-seven times" speaks not of our strength, but of God's.

A Moment to Reflect
- Think about the events of the day for a few moments before you go to sleep tonight. Do you remember a particular instance when you needed to forgive or receive forgiveness? Tell God about it.
- Make a point of watching the news. Ask yourself: Is there anything I can do—perhaps especially in prayer—to bring peace to one corner of the world?

A Moment to Pray
Lord Jesus, help me to grow in forgiveness. Make me a channel of your peace. St. Teresa of Calcutta, pray for us!

Wednesday of the Third Week of Lent
LIMITS THAT FREE US

Deuteronomy 4:1, 5–9; Psalm 147:12–13, 15–16, 19–20; Matthew 5:17–19

> But take care and watch yourselves closely, so as neither to forget the things that your eyes have seen nor to let them slip from your mind all the days of your life; make them known to your children and your children's children.
>
> —Deuteronomy 4:9

When a family opens their home to a foster child, teaching the new child the household routine can be a challenge. "No food in the bedroom" may seem like a perfectly reasonable rule...until you encounter a child who hoards produce and cheese because he doesn't know when the next meal will be. "Brush your teeth before bed" seems like a benign request...until you discover that not only does the child not own a toothbrush, but he eats toothpaste right out of the tube.

Experienced foster parents discover early on the importance of building simple but unshakable routines into each day, even posting them on charts with pictures—knowing full well that some flexibility is needed with children who are doing their best to cope in a new and possibly frightening environment. "See the pictures? First, let's get dressed. Then it's time to brush hair. Then time for breakfast—do you like cereal or eggs?"

In today's first reading, Moses tells the Hebrew people—former Egyptian slaves who have just evaded Pharaoh's army—about the Law of God. Many of them likely felt overwhelmed by their current situation, so far from the only home they had ever known. The people had followed Moses to freedom, but many families had long forgotten about Yahweh during their generations of captivity, and they did not immediately give up the idols and pagan traditions they had taken on.

This is why one of the first items on the agenda for Moses was to teach the people the Law and order them to teach the Ten Commandments to their children, to help them continually turn their hearts toward God. From these basic rules, the people eventually came to understand what it meant to live as the Chosen People—though the process took many years of wandering through the wilderness.

As Catholics, we have a similar responsibility to our children, whether they are ours by birth or by circumstance. Each time we bring them to Mass (instead of dropping them at CCD), lead them in praying the rosary, or have them recite passages from Scripture, we are strengthening relationships both vertical (between ourselves and God) and horizontal (among ourselves).

As the spiritual mother of her order, Mother Teresa carefully laid out what was expected of her Sisters and Co-Workers in order to help them prepare for the arduous work ahead. She also spent a great deal of time forming in her Sisters the virtue of simple obedience:

> If you want to know whether you love God, ask yourselves the question, "Do I obey?" If I obey, everything is alright. Why? Because everything depends on my will. Whether I become a saint or a sinner depends on me. So you see how very important obedience is.… Don't waste your time waiting for big things to do for God. You will not have the readiness to say yes to the great

things if you do not train yourselves to say yes to the thousand-and-one occasions of obedience that come your way throughout the day.[48]

For those on the outside, this training in obedience can at times appear to be heavy-handed or harsh. And yet, as human beings, we need to understand our place in the world. When that world is disturbed, we find peace by orienting ourselves toward some greater purpose and in relationship with those who share the journey.

A Moment to Reflect

- Did you encounter a situation today in which someone's "rule" seemed arbitrary or harsh? What might be another explanation?
- Is there a particular rule in your home or workplace that some routinely ignore? How might you respond in love?

A Moment to Pray

Almighty God, you brought the Chosen People out of slavery, but did not leave them to their own devices. You gave them limits, as a good father should, and taught them your ways. Help me to grow in the virtue of obedience, that I might grow closer to you. St. Teresa of Calcutta, pray for us!

Thursday of the Third Week of Lent
QUENCHING THIRSTY HEARTS

Jeremiah 7:23–28; Psalm 95:1–2, 6–7, 8–9; Luke 11:14–23

> From the day that your ancestors came out of the land of
> Egypt until this day, I have persistently sent all my servants and
> prophets to them, day after day; yet they did not listen to me, or
> pay attention, but they stiffened their necks.
>
> —Jeremiah 7:25–26

Have you ever known someone who desperately needed God or who was *this close* to becoming Catholic but simply refused to budge on a particular issue? For many people, the resistance often boils down to an unwillingness to surrender to a higher spiritual authority or to concede that they might need to let go of a deeply cherished idea. Sometimes it takes a miracle—but we believe in a God of miracles, a God who will stop at nothing to draw his beloved children to himself.

Mother Teresa believed that entrusting a person to the Blessed Mother is one of our most important weapons in the work of evangelization. She wrote, "How much we need Mary to teach us what it means to satiate God's thirsting Love for us, which Jesus came to reveal to us."[49] By entrusting the soul of our loved one into the keeping of the Blessed Mother and continuing to stand in faith with her, we make it possible for the Holy Spirit to speak directly to the heart of that person about the Lord's longing to draw the person to himself, just as he drew the Samaritan woman in Sunday's Gospel reading. Mother Teresa's friend Donna-Marie

Cooper O'Boyle explains:

> The Blessed Mother will teach us so much. Mother Teresa learned
> to stand with Mary at the foot of the cross, so very close to her
> Son, Jesus. There she listened with Mary to the painful cry of
> Jesus, "I thirst." Mary can help teach us how to quench Christ's
> thirst—his thirst for our love and the love of our family. Let us
> call upon Mary often for help with raising our families and for
> guidance in getting closer and closer to Jesus.[50]

As someone who became Catholic as an adult, I find the religious divisions between Jews and Samaritans, highlighted in the Gospel story of the Samaritan woman, similar to those I've witnessed among various Christian groups on both sides of the Tiber. Brothers and sisters in Christ do not always seem to recognize one another, let alone love one another.

Yet in his final days on earth, Jesus poured out to the Father his deep desire for unity among those who believe. "I ask not only on behalf of these, but also on behalf of those who will believe in me through their word, that they may all be one...as we are one" (John 17:20–22). A thirst even greater than the one he sought to quench in the soul of that Samaritan woman remains in his body, the Church, today.

In today's first reading, the prophetic words of Jeremiah give us an idea of just how long the Samaritans had been "stiff-necked" and set in their ways, which adds richness to the story about Jesus and the Samaritan woman. Think about it: Jesus doesn't go to one of the priests at the Samaritan temple. Instead he approaches the lonely woman drawing water from a public well, someone who, because of the circumstances of her life, is not too proud to acknowledge the thirst within her spirit:

Jesus said to her, "Everyone who drinks of this water will be thirsty again, but those who drink of the water that I will give them will never be thirsty. The water that I will give will become in them a spring of water gushing up to eternal life." The woman said to him, "Sir, give me this water, so that I may never be thirsty or have to keep coming here to draw water" (John 4:13–15).

A few moments later, Jesus reveals himself to be the promised Messiah (John 4:26). For the first time, the woman's eyes are opened to the liberating truth—that God loves her even in her brokenness. She drops everything to go share the news with the very neighbors she had been so determined to avoid (John 4:28–29). And she knows she will never be thirsty again.

A Moment to Reflect
- Think of a family member or friend with whom you've been wanting to talk about spiritual things. Have you been praying for an opportunity? Have you entrusted the person to the Blessed Mother, as St. Teresa suggested?
- What is one thing you could do tomorrow to "test the waters" with this person? Is there an event at church, a book you can recommend, or some other way to connect with this person God has placed on your heart?

A Moment to Pray
Blessed Mother, from the cross your Son gave you to us, to be our spiritual mother and to intercede for us as any good mother would. Thank you for praying for me and my loved ones, drawing us ever closer to Jesus. St. Teresa of Calcutta, pray for us!

Friday of the Third Week of Lent
SELF-SACRIFICING LOVE
Hosea 14:2–10; Psalm 8:6c–8a, 8bc–9, 10–11ab, 14, 17; Mark 12:28b–34

"Which commandment is the first of all?" Jesus answered, "The first is, 'Hear, O Israel: the Lord our God, the Lord is one; you shall love the Lord your God with all your heart, and with all your soul, and with all your mind, and with all your strength.' The second is this, 'You shall love your neighbor as yourself.' There is no other commandment greater than these."

—Mark 12:28b–31

In his book *A Revolution of Love,* David Scott records an interview with Mother Teresa in which she describes the heart-breaking plight of couples who conceived a child after contracting Hansen's disease (leprosy). Medical protocol dictated that the couple automatically relinquish the child for adoption, to prevent their infecting the infant with the disease. Mother Teresa on one occasion had to take an infant who was just three days old.

I cannot forget the deep love of that father and mother for their little child. I took the child, and I could see the father and mother as I was walking.... The agony and pain it caused!... But because they loved the child more than they loved themselves, they gave it up.[51]

While all parents are called to make sacrifices for their children, this level of self-sacrifice is nothing short of breathtaking. These loving parents could not save themselves through their actions, but they could make sure that their child would live.

In today's Gospel, Jesus reveals the transforming power of self-sacrificing love. Steadfast, unselfish love of God and those around us compels us to give ourselves wholeheartedly, out of a simple desire to seek the good of the beloved. And once we have given ourselves in this way, love compels us to hold on through even the most difficult circumstances.

When love is tainted with selfishness, it can inflict great damage. "Love can be misused for selfish motives," observed Mother Teresa. "I love you, but at the same time I want to take from you as much as I can, even the things that are not for me to take. Then there is no true love anymore."[52]

This selfish love is what we find in Sunday's Gospel of the Samaritan woman, who has been used and tossed aside and whose desperate search for love has led only to shame and ostracism. "I have no husband," she admits to Jesus. "You are right," Jesus responds (John 4:17). But he does not stop there. He loves her too much to leave her in her shame and ignorance. And so he kindly speaks the truth to her and shows her what true love looks like by challenging her—gently and lovingly—to face the truth about herself and her life choices. She cannot know how high a price the Messiah would pay for her liberation. All she knows is that standing right in front of her is One who perfectly embodies Love at its purest and best. And she cannot contain her joy: "Come and see a man who told me everything I have ever done! He cannot be the Messiah, can he?" (John 4:29).

On this Friday in Lent, we are called to respond in love to Love, to undertake some act of penance. We do so not out of a sense of grudging duty, but in an effort to open ourselves more completely to God and prepare ourselves for the holiest week of the Church year, when we remember the Father who sacrificed his own Son so that we might be redeemed.

"Love the Lord your God with all your heart, and with all your soul, and with all your mind, and with all your strength.... Love your neighbor as yourself."

Help me, Lord, to embrace this call anew.

A Moment to Reflect

- How did you express your love for God today? Would someone who knew you only casually have been able to tell you are a follower of Jesus?
- What is one way you can demonstrate the other part of the great commandment, to love your neighbor as yourself?

A Moment to Pray

Dearest Jesus, how often I've fallen short of loving you with everything I am, everything I have. And how often my love for my neighbor has been cold and conditional. Send your Spirit to fill my heart until it is on fire with love for you. St. Teresa of Calcutta, pray for us!

Saturday of the Third Week of Lent
TURN TOWARD THE LIGHT
Hosea 6:1–6; Psalm 51:3–4, 18–19, 20–21ab; Luke 18:9–14

For I know my transgressions,
    and my sin is ever before me. Against you, you alone, have I
sinned,
    and done what is evil in your sight, so that you are justified in
your sentence
    and blameless when you pass judgment.

—Psalm 51:3–4

This week we have reflected upon the story of the Samaritan woman who encounters Jesus at the well. Though she has sinned and been sinned against greatly, Jesus regards her with the greatest, most tender mercy. He sees that she has been damaged and thus does not heap shame upon shame by treating her harshly. Instead he holds up the truth like a warm light and invites her to see herself not just for who she has been, but for who she was made to be.

Mother Teresa and her Sisters embodied this same tenderness, making no demands and forming no harsh judgments on those to whom they ministered. Rather, they simply radiated the infinite mercy and love of God. And people responded, sometimes in spite of themselves.

One night Mother Teresa appeared on a Canadian television program with two famous French scientists, one a practicing Christian and the other a molecular biologist and atheist who had recently won a Nobel Prize and who believed that "the destiny of man is inexorably locked up in his genes." The two scientists debated about the meaning of human existence for some time and finally asked Mother Teresa what she thought.

"I believe in love and compassion," she said.[53]

This conviction of St. Teresa's, lived out each day in countless acts of love, had a transforming effect on those who worked with or even just visited her. One well-known photographer was taking pictures at Nirmal Hriday, the home for the dying destitute, when he came across an old woman who was not in her right mind; she mistook him for her own son. When she called to him, he found himself unable to disappoint her and, taking her hand gently in his own, responded, "Yes, Mother. I'm here."

The woman died happy, and later the photographer couldn't wait to find Mother Teresa and tell her of the transcendent effect of that experience. "I did not believe in God…but today I do."[54]

I often marvel at St. Teresa's ability to endure the most relentless demands, tirelessly traveling all over the world to tend to the needs of her many spiritual daughters and Co-Workers as well as hundreds of thousands of those who had been beaten down by poverty and illness. No one would have blamed her had she, out of simple self-preservation, resorted to shielding herself from the worst of it.

Instead, she reflected the love of God so brightly and so continuously that even those who knew themselves to be far from God, like the photographer, could not help but take a few steps closer, attracted by the warmth and the light. These are the first steps on the journey toward conversion, the process by which the soul willingly relinquishes all that is holding it back from love. It is a frank acknowledgment of who we are now (as laid out in today's psalm), who we need to become, and our utter dependence on the grace of God to get us safely there.

A Moment to Reflect

- What part of the story of the Samaritan woman at the well most resonates with you? (If necessary, reread the account in John 4:1–30.)
- Is there an area of your life that you sense God is asking you to turn over to him? What can you do today to move toward that place of conversion?

A Moment to Pray

Father God, you have made me to know and to love you— and yet you know all too well how imperfect I am and how far I have to go. Give me the courage to deal gently with those who need your mercy, even myself. St. Teresa of Calcutta, pray for us!

Fourth Week of Lent
BE HEALED

Fourth Sunday of Lent
BLIND ASSUMPTIONS

Year A: 1 Samuel 16:1b, 6–7, 10–13; Psalm 23:1–3a, 3b–4, 5, 6;
Ephesians 5:8–14; John 9:1–41
Year B: 2 Chronicles 36:14–16, 19–23;Psalm 137:1–2, 3, 4–5, 6;
Ephesians 2:4–10; John 3:14–21
Year C: Joshua 5:9a, 10–12; Psalm 34:2–3, 4–5, 6–7;
2 Corinthians 5:17–21; Luke 15:1–3, 11–32

As [Jesus] walked along, he saw a man blind from birth. His
disciples asked him, "Rabbi, who sinned, this man or his parents,
that he was born blind?" Jesus answered, "Neither this man nor
his parents sinned; he was born blind so that God's works might
be revealed in him."

—John 9:1–3

In *Thirsting for God*, Mother Teresa recalls that the grandson of Malcolm
Muggeridge, an evangelical Christian pastor, told her, "Mother Teresa, I

like everything I see, I like what you do, I like you, yet there is something I do not understand: You are so full of Mary." Mother replied simply, "No mother, no son. Without Mary, there would be no Jesus." The story continues: "Much time had passed when I received a postcard with, in capital letters, 'No mother, no son: I understood; this has changed my life.'"[55]

It is human nature to hold tight to what is familiar and to judge those whose experiences and beliefs rub uncomfortably against our own. Like the pastor in this story, I grew up with certain faith-based biases against Catholicism that I accepted uncritically. Looking back, I can see that God put certain people in my path who, little by little, helped me to appreciate the full beauty and truth contained within the Catholic Church. Some of them gave me books and tapes, but most of them were simply loving, patient Catholics who absorbed the critical and even hurtful things I sometimes said. Instead of arguing back, they just came alongside me and let me see them for who they truly were: fellow followers of Christ.

One of those patient souls gave me a Miraculous Medal sometime after my confirmation. I had moved halfway across the country, far from my home parish, and Mass had become a lonely hour. Knowing that a relationship with the Blessed Mother was still a question mark for me, this friend simply invited me to "tell Mary about it."

Reluctantly, I decided to try her approach. The first Sunday I apologized to God in advance—in case he had a problem with what I was about to do—and then blurted out, "Mary-if-you-can-hear-me-I'd-like-someone-to-sit-with-me-at-Mass-today-Amen." Entering the church, I found a seat and knelt down to pray...and when I looked up I saw a woman I didn't recognize standing next to me. "Hi. I just moved into town and don't know anyone. Can I sit with you?"

Coincidence, I thought. But I gladly slid over to make room for her.

The second week I eyed the medal resting on the passenger seat of my car. "That wasn't funny, God," I told him. "If it happens again this week, I'm going to think there is something to this. Mary-please-send-someone-to-sit-with-me-Amen."

Another stranger appeared at my pew—another bit of light. When it happened again the following week, I could no longer ignore the message. Yes, Mary cared. Yes, she could hear me. Yes, she wanted to help. By the time I became a mother myself a few years later, calling out to her for help had become as natural as breathing: "Mary, you were the perfect mother with one perfect Son. I don't have either of those things going for me.... HELP!" I had not been raised to think of Jesus's mother in that way, but over time my eyes had been opened to see and welcome her motherly intervention.

In today's Gospel narrative, Jesus brings sight to a man "blind from birth"; he spits on some dirt and rubs it on the man's eyes and then instructs him to wash off in the ritual pool. The grittiness of the scene is a bit shocking (why *spit?*). But then, is it any more shocking than his offering up his very Body and Blood to infuse us with his own life, to make us ready for heaven?

Those who witness the man's healing are full of questions. Who has done this, and why? What does it mean? When God wants to take the blinders from our eyes in order to heal and transform us—whether physically or spiritually—we must be ready to embrace the experience in all its gritty mystery. At some point in our lives, we all must decide whether to hold on to past beliefs and wounds, clinging blindly and uncritically to the familiar, or to accept the illumination God wants to give all his children.

A Moment to Reflect

- Is there an area of your life in which you suffer from "blind assumptions"? Are you ready to receive God's healing through the sacraments?
- Ask God to illuminate your mind, making you aware of any areas of willful blindness in your life—issues of compromise or resistance to the light of truth.

A Moment to Pray

O God of truth and light, examine my heart and open my eyes. Help me to recognize and let go of anything that is displeasing to you or that puts a barrier between us. Blessed Mother, pray for me that I might not be afraid to see the truth. St. Teresa of Calcutta, pray for us!

Monday of the Fourth Week of Lent
HEALING FAITH
Isaiah 65:17–21; Psalm 30:2, 4, 5–6, 11–12a, 13b; John 4:43–54

The official said to him, "Sir, come down before my little boy dies." Jesus said to him, "Go; your son will live." The man believed the word that Jesus spoke to him and started on his way. As he was going down, his slaves met him and told him that his child was alive.

—John 4:49–51

In the three years of his public ministry, Jesus worked many different kinds of miracles, from his first at the wedding of Cana, where he turned water into wine (see John 2:1–11), to moments before his arrest, when he restored the severed ear of the high priest's slave (see Luke 22:51). In yesterday's Gospel narrative, Jesus healed a blind man with mud made from Jesus's own saliva, an intimate healing experience that dramatically changed the course of the man's life.

In today's Gospel, we encounter a very different kind of healing, in which the son of a Roman official is healed from a distance, with the healing pronounced to the boy's father. This healing seems less "personal" because of the lack of physical proximity, and yet a closer look at the story reveals that Jesus knew exactly what sort of miracle would speak to that particular family: the Scriptures tell us that because the boy was healed from afar, the boy's father believed "along with his whole household" (John 4:53).

For Mother Teresa, this personal sense of encounter was indispensable to the work she did among the poor, for it broke through the sense of isolation and marginalization that marked their lives, and reminded them of their personal dignity. In *A Simple Path*, Brother Geoff, MC, General Servant of Missionaries of Charity Brothers, captures this intentional connection beautifully:

> When people who are used to being rejected and abandoned experience being accepted by others and being loved, when they see people are giving of their time and energy for them, that conveys a message that, after all, they are not rubbish.
>
> Certainly, love is expressed first in being with before doing to someone. We…can get caught up in a lot of the doing for…. Service, in a way, is simply a means of expressing your being for that person—and often with the poorest people you cannot completely alleviate their problem. But by being with them, by being for them, whatever you can do for them makes a difference.[56]

How can we begin to bring comfort and encouragement through the simple gift of personal connection, even in situations when it cannot solve the root of the problem? Brother Geoff's reflection reminds me of my own mother, who for four years went each week to visit a friend with Lou Gehrig's disease (ALS). Every Wednesday after Bible study, Mom would stop by to see Rosemary and her children and do some of the motherly things that the sick woman was no longer able to do herself. As the disease progressed and eventually robbed Rosemary of her capacity to move and even to speak, many of her other visitors stopped coming, unsure of what to say and unwilling to confront the fact that their prayers for healing had apparently gone unanswered. But my mother kept visiting, and I admired her dogged persistence in continuing to find ways to keep that connection with her friend.

Toward the end, when the only volitional action remaining to Rosemary was blinking her eyes, Mom had a special way to pinpoint each letter of a word her friend wanted to convey by the number and timing of her blinks; her method included dividing the alphabet into four key words: AldolF (A–F), GirL (G–L), ManneR (M–R), and StaY (S–Z). Mom would breeze into the room and say, "My, you're looking so rested today, dear! Is there anything I can get you? Let's see…two blinks: yes. Good! What's the first letter? Aldolf, girl, manner, stay: Stay? Okay, what letter? S-T-U-V-W: Starts with W. Do you want water? Two blinks? I'll be right back!" She would moisten the woman's lips, then sit down and read to her for an hour while in the kitchen we dived into the care package of cookies with Rosemary's children. Mom always brought them, knowing that the kids needed a break from their grief, too.

"Aunt" Rosemary did not recover as all her friends prayed she would. And yet I believed she experienced the healing touch of God through my mother's gift of presence.

A Moment to Reflect

- At any point in your day, did you give the "gift of presence" to someone who needed it?
- Think about how you might offer someone a healing touch, either physically (as Mother Teresa often did) or from a distance (as Jesus did in today's Gospel), through a personal note or phone call.

A Moment to Pray

Holy Spirit, show me how I can better bring God's gift of healing touch to the world around me. Help me to see the needs, and give me wisdom to respond. St. Teresa of Calcutta, pray for us!

Tuesday of the Fourth Week of Lent
Do You Want to Be Well?
Ezekiel 47:1–9, 12; Psalm 46:2–3, 5–6, 8–9; John 5:1–3a, 5–16

One man was there who had been ill for thirty-eight years. When Jesus saw him lying there and knew that he had been there a long time, he said to him, "Do you want to be made well?"

—John 5:5–6

"What does it mean when the Church refers to penance and anointing as 'sacraments of healing'? Have you ever witnessed someone receiving physical healing through the sacraments?" When I posed these questions to my seminary professor, he looked a bit startled. Judging from his reaction, not many of his students had experienced a direct "faith healing."

I had experienced it on one occasion, as a Protestant. A metal pin that had been inserted in my leg after my car accident a year earlier had worked itself loose and was digging painfully into my hip joint. One day before the pin was to be surgically removed, a deacon and his wife from the campus church asked God to heal me, and the pin spontaneously moved to its rightful place. Although I was grateful for the cessation of pain, the experience had raised uncomfortable questions in my mind. Why would God grant a miracle in this case, when all over the world people with conditions far more serious than mine continued to suffer and die? It wasn't until I became Catholic and began to understand, thanks to the patient teaching of my seminary professor, how God uses suffering to perfect us in holiness that I was able to put these questions to rest. For reasons best known to him, God had seen that the healing I needed most was not my hip but my heart; by granting me physical healing, he had challenged me to embrace the goodness of my heavenly Father, whose wisdom far surpasses my own.

Still, reading through the stories of St. Teresa, I am struck by the miraculous ways God answered her prayers at times. On one occasion, moments after a Sister notified her that they had no food to feed the people for breakfast, Mother Teresa prayed and a bread truck mysteriously appeared at their door.[57] On another occasion, a dying infant was restored to health the day after Mother Teresa took the little one in her arms and offered an Our Father.[58] She and her Sisters tended to thousands of sick and destitute souls every day, and many died—but many lived as well. Fortified by the power of the Eucharist, the Sisters' prayers worked miracles.

Miracles didn't happen every day, of course. When the work became too overwhelming, the burden too great, Mother Teresa would remind her Sisters that just as prayer lightens the load, the lack of it can have the opposite effect:

> We are called to live the love of God, not to feel the love of God. We live this love through prayer and action. Our work is the fruit of our prayer, so that if our work is not going well, we must examine our prayer life. If we neglect our work or are harsh, proud, moody, and angry, then we should examine our prayer life.[59]

The prayer of surrender is at the heart of today's Gospel reading, in which Jesus heals an invalid who had been lying by the healing pool of Bethzatha for nearly four decades. For thirty-eight years the man had sought healing. With many others who were also in need, he had waited to be the first person to enter the waters after the angels stirred them, infusing them with healing power. Somehow his time had never come; someone always beat him to the water. "Do you want to be made well?" Jesus asks him. After so long a time, is he ready for a new and independent chapter of his life to begin? Would he surrender to the mystery?

Jesus's question to the man by the pool resonates in us as well. Whether the healing we need most is physical or spiritual, the question is the same. "Do you want to be made well?" Are you in need of the sacraments of healing? Are you willing to work? Are you willing to ask for what you need, and to make the effort necessary to obtain those graces? Are you willing to "stand up, take your mat and walk" (John 5:8)? And once you have received that healing, will you listen to Jesus, who says: "See, you have been made well! Do not sin anymore, so that nothing worse happens to you" (John 5:14).

> Dear Lord, the Great Healer.... Give me singleness of purpose, strength to lift up a part of the burden of my suffering fellowmen, and a realization of the privilege that is mine. Take from my heart all guile and worldliness, that with the simple faith of a child, I may rely on you. Amen.[60]

A Moment to Reflect

- Was there a moment today when you found yourself feeling "harsh, proud, moody, or angry"? Do you need to ask God to heal whatever is causing these weeds to flourish in the garden of your heart?
- Think about how you can connect prayer and work more deliberately in your daily life. Do you entrust each workday to God and ask him

to guide and multiply your efforts? Do you offer him successes and setbacks alike, asking him to use both to help you grow in holiness?

A Moment to Pray

Lord Jesus, thank you for the work you have given me to do. Thank you for the people you have put in my life with whom I can work and pray. Today I invite you to look in my heart and show me where I most need your healing. St. Teresa of Calcutta, pray for us!

Wednesday of the Fourth Week of Lent
UNFORGETTABLE
Isaiah 49:8–15; Psalm 145:8–9, 13cd–14, 17–18; John 5:17–30

But Zion said, "The Lord has forsaken me,
    my Lord has forgotten me." Can a woman forget her nursing child,
    or show no compassion for the child of her womb? Even these may forget,
    yet I will not forget you.

—Isaiah 49:14–15

When Mother Teresa received her "call within a call" in 1946 on the train to Darjeeling, the Lord was very clear about the work he had given her to do: "I was to leave the convent and work with the poor, living among them. It was an order. I knew where I belonged but I did not know how to get there."[61]

Mother Teresa: Come Be My Light captures in detail her discernment process, which involved extensive correspondence between Mother Teresa, her spiritual director Jesuit Father Celeste Van Exem, the superiors of her religious order, and the Jesuit archbishop of Calcutta, Ferdinand Périer. Although she submitted to her spiritual director's requirement that she be patient, Mother Teresa was eager to undertake the work she knew God had given her, to satiate Jesus's thirst for souls by bringing his love to the poor. In one of the letters, she recorded the Lord's pleading words to her:

Little one, give Me souls—Give me the souls of the poor little street children.—How it hurts, if you only knew, to see these poor children soiled with sin.—I long for the purity of their love—If you would only answer and bring me these souls—draw them away from the hands of the evil one. If you only knew how many little ones fall into sin every day. There are plenty of Nuns to look after the rich and the well to do people—but for My very poor, there are absolutely none. For them I long—them I love. Wilt thou refuse?[62]

Today's Old Testament reading touches upon the longing God has for his children, comparing it to the love a mother has for her children. The Scriptures of the New Testament speak of us as God's children by adoption (see Ephesians 1:5; Romans 8:15–16). For God, each human soul is unrepeatable, irreplaceable, unforgettable.

But it is easy for us—caught up in the regrets of the past, the demands of the present, and the worries of the future—to lose sight of just how great is the love of our Father's heart. Even Mother Teresa experienced the desolation of not being able to sense the nearness of God for much of her life. Yet she labored on in love for and obedience to the One to whom she had pledged her life, never ceasing to reassure the souls who most needed to hear the joyful words of God's unfailing love for them.

Jesus wants me to tell you again…how much is the love He has for each one of you—beyond all what you can imagine.… Not only he loves you, even more—He longs for you. He misses you when you don't come close. He thirsts for you. He loves you always, even when you don't feel worthy.[63]

A Moment to Reflect

• Do you believe that you are "unforgettable" to God? Do you believe that he longs to be near you, longs to hear you speak to him with love and trust?

• Who in your life most needs to hear the message that God has not forgotten him or her? How will you share this message with the person?

A Moment to Pray

St. Teresa, for years you toiled in the shadows, unable to feel the light of Christ's presence even as you brought that light to others. Pray for me, that I would not give up in discouragement but continue to love the God who longs to be with me. St. Teresa of Calcutta, pray for us!

Thursday of the Fourth Week of Lent
LAYING DOWN THE GOLDEN CALF
Exodus 32:7–14; Psalm 106:19–20, 21–22, 23; John 5:31–47

> And the Lord changed his mind about the disaster that he
> planned to bring on his people.
>
> —Exodus 32:14

In today's first reading, we find the Chosen People of God having fallen
into apostasy. Moses is still up on the mountain communing with God on
behalf of his people when trouble erupts on the plain below. The Hebrews
have grown tired of waiting, and some are afraid that Moses will never
return, leaving them unprotected. And so they demand that his brother,
the high priest Aaron, fill the void by creating a god they can see and
touch (Exodus 32:1). Amazingly, Aaron gives in to their demands, and
casts a golden calf for them.[64]

God is understandably outraged and threatens to destroy the Hebrews
(32:10). Moses intercedes for the people so eloquently that the Lord relents
(32:14). And yet they do not entirely escape judgment: Moses burns the
calf, turns it into a powder, and tosses it into the Israelites' drinking water
(32:19–20), and Aaron is blamed: "for Aaron had let [the people] run,
to the derision of their enemies" (32:25). This void in leadership yields
devastating results: at Moses' command, the Levites take up weapons and
slaughter three thousand of their own people to make atonement for the
sacrilege (32:27–29).

This story has sobering implications for those in positions of leadership
—pastors, teachers, and parents included. When we fail to model for and

teach those who have been entrusted into our care, the devastation can have wide-reaching effects. And if we do not maintain our own connection with God through prayer and the sacraments, we cannot hope to remain strong in our ability to lead. Those who look to us for leadership will falter. And from there, it's only a matter of time before the evil one lures them away. We see this in Aaron, who lost his spiritual power while Moses was up on the mountain—he was so busy attending to the demands of leadership, he forgot to pray.

Mother Teresa knew prayer was an indispensable lifeline for the difficult work she and her Sisters had been called to do because it kept them in close contact with the One they loved most. She frequently admonished her Sisters not to neglect their time in prayer and Adoration:

> Our vocation is the conviction that "I belong to him." Because I belong to him, he must be free to use me. I must surrender completely. When we look at his cross, we understand his love. His head is bent down to kiss us. His hands are extended to embrace us. His heart is wide open to receive us. That is what we have to be in the world today. We, too, must have our head bent down to our people—to the school, where we are teaching or to the sick and dying destitute that we are helping. This is Jesus in his distressing disguise. Whether in the school or in the slum, it is the same Jesus.[65]

Think for a moment about how this applies to your situation. We who have not been called to the priesthood or to a religious vocation still belong to God; we can still derive peace and strength by acknowledging both the limits of our own resources and our dependence on the Lord. The golden calf takes many forms—whatever you possess can ultimately possess you, if you do not attend to the life of the spirit. Have you surrendered yourself completely into God's hands and professed your trust in him?

A Moment to Reflect

- Can you think of a time when you found it difficult to trust God? Did you come up with your own "golden calf" to solve the problem? How did Mother Teresa's advice apply to your situation?
- If you have been reluctant to admit your dependence on God, what is holding you back? Consider talking to a priest or spiritual director if you are unsure.

A Moment to Pray

Almighty Trinity, you are the one and only true God. I worship and adore you alone, and I trust you absolutely to meet my needs and the needs of my family. Forgive me when I take shortcuts or disobey you even in the small details of my life. Thank you for your abundant mercy, which makes me strong again. St. Teresa of Calcutta, pray for us!

Friday of the Fourth Week of Lent
THE NEED TO BE KNOWN
Wisdom 2:1a, 12–22; Psalm 34:17–18, 19–20, 21, 23; John 7:1–2, 10, 25–30

> Then Jesus cried out as he was teaching in the temple, "You
> know me, and you know where I am from. I have not come on
> my own. But the one who sent me is true, and you do not know
> him."
>
> —John 7:28

In *A Simple Path,* Sister Dolores, MC, speaks of the great loneliness that
causes so many people in New York City to seek out the Missionaries of
Charity—not simply for the food, but to meet a different urgent need:

> In the West there is so much loneliness. Most lonely people just
> need someone to sit with them, be with them, smile at them,
> because many do not have any family left and are living alone,
> are shut in. So on different occasions during the year…we would
> bring these people all together…so they could meet others.…
> We'd give them a good lunch and some cakes—and just by
> having them come out of their homes and mix with others we
> brought happiness into their lives.[66]

Today's Gospel is set during the Jewish Feast of Booths, or Sukkoth, an
autumnal feast of thanksgiving that also commemorates the forty-year
journey of the Exodus. During this feast, the Jews would live in small,
temporary shelters or booths commemorating God's protection and
provision.

At this particular feast, Jesus walks a tenuous line between revealing himself to those who need to hear his message of salvation and protecting himself from those who seek to do him harm, for "My time has not yet come" (John 7:6). All around him, people are clamoring for the Messiah— yet they are unable to recognize the one they seek in this Nazarene who shows up in the middle of the festival and begins to teach (7:14).

In Sunday's meditation, we examined the story of Jesus healing the man born blind, and today we encounter the Lord once more trying to restore sight, this time the sight of those who clamor in the Temple courtyard, unable to see the Messiah standing right in front of them. Imagine for a moment what that must have been like for Jesus. Imagine how much strength it must have taken for him to persevere, knowing that his own people would never recognize the miracle of God's provision standing in their midst.

Consider the loneliness of Christ. "You know me!" Jesus cries out. "You know where I am from…. The one who sent me is true, and you do not know him" (John 7:28). And yet, not even his "brothers" believe Jesus— or wanted to protect him from those who wished him ill: they tell him, "If you do these things, show yourself to the world" (7:4).

On Fridays in Lent, we make our small acts of sacrifice or abstinence not because we think it makes us better than others, but because it is an opportunity to stand with Jesus, to identify with his lonely passion in a very practical and personal way. In the words of Mother Teresa:

> We feed ourselves, not to please our senses, but to show our Lord that we want to work for him and with him, to live a life of sacrifice and reparation.[67]

One of the ways we can put these words into very deliberate practice is through participating in communal acts of thanksgiving and penance, especially through our own parish. (If there are no fish fries or soup suppers offered at your parish, consider volunteering to organize such an event!) Through this intentional practice of the gift of hospitality, we can build up the sense of community and connection and meet the needs of the lonely and marginalized. However, the most important reason for us to gather together is to stand with Jesus, offering ourselves to him not just when it's convenient, but whenever we become aware of his lonely heart's cry.

A Moment to Reflect

- What did you "offer up" to Jesus, or how did you stand with him today? How do you feel when you think about the loneliness of Christ?
- What is one thing you can do this weekend to stand with the lonely of your community or parish?

A Moment to Pray

Lord Jesus, you gave up all of heaven in order to show me the way to God. Let me stand with you and love you, dear Savior. Please accept the small offerings that I have for you today, and know that I give them with all the love of my heart. St. Teresa of Calcutta, pray for us!

Saturday of the Fourth Week of Lent

AN INCONVENIENT TRUTH

Jeremiah 11:18–20; Psalm 7:2–3, 9bc–10, 11–12; John 7:40–53

The Lord judges the peoples;
> judge me, O Lord, according to my righteousness
> and according to the integrity that is in me.

—Psalm 7:8

In today's Gospel reading, the leaders of the Temple send the Temple police to arrest Jesus. They see in Jesus a dangerous man, especially because of his effect on crowds: some people follow him, hoping for another miracle; others listen, fascinated, to his teachings; still others see in him the promised Messiah. This last group, the Pharisees realize, is the most dangerous of all—those calling him the Messiah could create yet another insurrection that would bring all of Rome rushing in to restore order. No, this Galilean must be silenced.

But when the Temple police go out to do their duty, they become enamored with the message of Jesus: "Never has anyone spoken like this!" (John 7:46). And so they return to the Temple empty-handed. They do not know who Jesus is, but they recognize the power of his message.

In the same way, said Mother Teresa, we must introduce Christ to those who do not know him so they recognize the power of his message.

> Let us preach the peace of Christ like he did; he went about doing good. He did not stop his works of charity because the Pharisees and others hated him or tried to spoil his Father's work. He just went about doing good. Cardinal Newman wrote:

"Help me to spread thy fragrance everywhere I go; let me preach thee without preaching, not by words but by my example—by the catching force, the sympathetic influence of what I do, the evident fullness of the love my heart bears to thee." Our works of love are nothing but works of peace. Let us do them with greater love and efficiency.

It is always the same Christ who says:

I was hungry—not only for food, but for peace that comes from a pure heart.

I was thirsty—not for water, but for peace that satiates that passionate thirst of passion for war.

I was naked—not for clothes, but for the beautiful dignity of men and women for their bodies.

I was homeless—not for a shelter made of bricks, but for a heart that understands, that covers, that loves.[68]

The Pharisees and other leaders in the Temple had heard Jesus proclaim the same words the people heard, and yet they did not respond the same way. Where the people heard a prophet and recognized the authority with which he spoke—regardless of where he came from—the chief priests and Pharisees had a vested interest in dismissing Jesus. Because of the hatred of the others, the Pharisee Nicodemus, who by that time was a secret follower of Jesus, was unwilling to defend Jesus overtly. He merely protested Jesus's arrest on a technicality: "Our law does not judge people without first giving them a hearing to find out what they are doing, does it?" (John 7:50–51). Even this bloodless defense subjected Nicodemus to scorn and derision.

And so it is today. To be a follower of Jesus is to rankle the status quo, to speak a language that often falls on deaf ears. Speaking the truth kindly and "spreading the fragrance" are necessary parts of the Christian life… but we will also be thorns in the side of anyone who seeks to silence inconvenient truth.

The question, then, becomes a simple one: whose judgment matters most?

A Moment to Reflect

- When was the last time you spoke an inconvenient truth? In retrospect, is there anything you wish you'd done differently?
- In what part of your life do you most need to "spread the fragrance" of Jesus? Is it time to make a change?

A Moment to Pray

Lord Jesus, you were never afraid to speak the truth, even to those who thought they already had a corner on it. Though they abused you for it, you continued to challenge them in love. Help me, Lord, to find the courage to follow your example. St. Teresa of Calcutta, pray for us!

Fifth Week of Lent
RAISED TO NEW LIFE

Fifth Sunday of Lent
FAMILY REUNION

Year A: Ezekiel 37:12–14; Psalm 130:1–2, 3–4, 5–6, 7–8
Romans 8:8–11; John 11:1–45
Year B: Jeremiah 31:31–34; Psalm 51: 3–4, 12–13, 14–15;
Hebrews 5:7–9; John 12:20–33
Year C: Isaiah 43:16–21; Psalm 126:1–2a, 2b–3, 4–5, 6;
Philippians 3:8–14; John 8:1–11

Martha said to him, "I know that he will rise again in the resurrection on the last day." Jesus said to her, "I am the resurrection and the life. Those who believe in me, even though they die, will live…."

—John 11:24–25

In their book *Suffering into Joy,* the Egan sisters write about the moment in 1960 when Eileen Egan accompanied Mother Teresa to Rome to request official recognition of the Missionaries of Charity. In Rome, after a separation of more than thirty years, Mother Teresa was finally reunited with her brother Lazar (Lazarus) and his family. The Egans write:

> Mother Teresa had appealed to Albanian officials for visas for her mother and sister, but the country was sealed off from the rest of Europe and would issue no visas for the women. Mother never saw them again, but knew they would be reunited one day. "We will meet in heaven. When I go home to God, for death is nothing else than going home to God, the bond of love will be unbroken for all eternity."[69]

Mother Teresa's profound understanding of the nature of death was undoubtedly providential in the work with the dying that God entrusted to her. Perhaps it was her early encounter with death that caused Mother Teresa to live with heaven on her mind. Born Agnes Bojaxhiu, she was only eight years old when she lost her own father in 1919. Having left home for work in perfect health, he was brought home in a carriage on the brink of death, hemorrhaging severely. The local hospital was unable to save him; many thought he had been poisoned.[70] No doubt this early trauma shaped the way she looked at the world, always with heaven in mind, and contributed to her decision at the age of twelve to become a nun and her joining the Loreto nuns as a novice at the age of eighteen.[71]

Memento mori (remember death) also characterized the mindset of the early Christians, many of whom were martyred for their beliefs. To the degree that we live each day in the shadow of eternity, we will invest our time and our lives in occupations that truly matter. For each of us, death is a doorway to something infinitely better and more lasting: a true family reunion, in which we will finally join all those who have been watching over us and praying for us as we made our journey heavenward!

In today's Gospel, Jesus hastens toward Bethany with his disciples to attend to their friend Lazarus, who has recently died, and to reveal himself as "the resurrection and the life" (John 11:25). By raising Lazarus from the dead, Jesus offers a sign not just to Lazarus but to all who witness the miracle—including us—that sin and death are only temporary. Our ultimate reality is still ahead of us—and it will be beautiful and joyous, so long as we live our earthly lives with our eternal destiny clearly in our sights.

A Moment to Reflect

- When you heard the Gospel proclaimed today, what struck you most about the story of Lazarus and his sisters?
- How might you follow in the example of St. Teresa and live with greater intentionality by embracing the call to *memento mori*?

A Moment to Pray

Heavenly Father, thank you for the gift of today. Help me to spend my time here on earth wisely, with eternity in view, so that at the end of my life you will welcome me with the saints in heaven. St. Teresa of Calcutta, pray for us!

Monday of the Fifth Week of Lent
BREAKING THE CYCLE OF VIOLENCE
Daniel 13:1–9, 15–17, 19–30, 33–62; Psalm 23:1–3a, 3b–4, 5, 6; John 8:1–11

When they kept on questioning him, he straightened up and
said to them, "Let anyone among you who is without sin be the
first to throw a stone at her."

—John 8:7

As a sophomore in high school, "Kim" had a promising future as a gifted
student and artist. Pretty and blonde, she made both top grades and friends
effortlessly. In her spare time, she designed her own clothes, including an
exquisite formal gown that she proudly wore to her first prom, which she
attended with a friend.

Then, in just a few short months, her world blew apart. She met "Dan,"
a senior. Flattered by the attention of an older student and sympathetic to
the sad stories he told about his home life, Kim was soon spending every
spare moment with him. Next she stopped wearing makeup and started
dressing in oversized and unflattering sportswear. She began to avoid her
friends and family and spent hours alone in her room, talking to Dan
on the phone. At one point she broke things off, but then Dan started
stalking her new boyfriend's family, and Kim wound up pregnant and
alone. Not seeing any other option, she married Dan.

It was then that the beatings began.

The nightmare continued for three years. Kim was a prisoner in her
own home when Dan was at work. He threatened to have her declared

unfit and take her baby if she ever tried to leave him, and because he had friends on the police force she was sure he'd make good on his threat. It wasn't until he threatened to kill her daughter that Kim found the strength to escape. Today she is a domestic abuse advocate helping women whose stories bear striking similarities to her own.

The unnamed woman in today's Gospel narrative reminds me a great deal of Kim and thousands of other abused women across the United States—unable to protect themselves from their abusers...or from the scrutiny and derision of the casual observer who does not see the invisible bars that keep them trapped in an unending cycle of violence, marginalization, and domination. Two of the strongest bars in this prison are poverty and isolation.

In the Heart of the World captures the wisdom of St. Teresa concerning the importance of leveling the playing field for those trapped in cycles of poverty and isolation—those who grow increasingly disheartened with each passing day, eventually despairing of ever being able to rise above their circumstances. They urgently need the compassionate intervention of someone with the courage to walk with them, and raise them up to new life, here and now.

> At a seminary in Bangalore, a nun once said to me, "Mother Teresa, you are spoiling the poor people by giving them things free. They are losing their human dignity."
>
> When everyone was quiet, I said calmly, "No one spoils as much as God himself. See the wonderful gifts He has given us freely. All of you here have no glasses, yet all of you can see. If God were to take money for your sight, what would happen?

Continually we are breathing and living on oxygen that we do not pay for. What would happen if God were to say, 'If you work for four hours, you get sunshine for two hours'? How many of us would survive then?"

Then I also told them, "There are many congregations that spoil the rich; it is good to have one congregation in the name of the poor, to spoil the poor." There was profound silence; nobody said a word after that.[72]

Just as Lazarus in Sunday's Gospel was unable to free himself from the bonds of his own grave clothes after Jesus raised him from the dead, the woman in today's Gospel needed assistance in breaking free from the circle of accusation and harsh judgment masquerading as "justice." When we, as followers of Christ, rise up to defend victims of poverty and violence, we are simply following the teachings of Christ: "Religion that is pure and undefiled before God, the Father, is this: to care for orphans and widows in their distress, and to keep oneself unstained by the world" (James 1:27).

A Moment to Reflect

- Do you know someone who you suspect could be a victim of domestic violence? If you would like information about how to help, contact the National Network to End Domestic Violence (nnedv.org) or The National Domestic Violence Hotline (ndvh.org).

- Have you read the United States Conference of Catholic Bishops' pastoral letter on domestic violence? It's called "When I Call for Help: A Pastoral Response to Domestic Violence Against Women."[73] Please read it.

A Moment to Pray

Heavenly Father, it is never your will that one of your children live in fear. Send your angels to deliver those caught up in the web of violence and despair, and show me how I can help. St. Teresa of Calcutta, pray for us!

Tuesday of the Fifth Week of Lent
DEFEND LIFE
Numbers 21:4–9; Psalm 102:2–3, 16–18, 19–21; John 8:21–30

Let this be recorded for a generation to come,
so that a people yet unborn may praise the Lord....
—Psalm 102:18

One of the subjects about which St. Teresa spoke most passionately was the value of every human life, including those yet to be born. In *No Greater Love,* she recounts a story that touches upon what for some is a dividing line of justice—the rights of children conceived in rape and those of their mothers. St. Teresa knew that the mothers must be protected from the trauma of abortion, which so often compounds rather than diminishes the trauma of rape.

> When we were invited to take care of the young women of Bangladesh who had been raped by soldiers, we saw the need to open a home for children. The difficulties were great because accepting in society young women who had been raped went against both Hindu and Muslim laws. But when the leader of Bangladesh said that those young women were heroines of the nation, who had fought for their own purity, who had struggled for their country, their very parents came to look for them.
>
> Some people favored abortion. I told the government that the young women had been violated, whereas what they wanted to do was force these women or help them commit a transgression

that would accompany them throughout their lives. Thanks be to God, the government accepted our conditions that each of the children for whom abortion would have been chosen should be taken to the house of Mother Teresa to receive help. Of the forty children we received, more than thirty went to Canada and other countries, adopted by generous families.[74]

For women who have experienced sexual assault, obtaining immediate medical attention in order to prevent conception can be helpful in restoring a sense of normalcy and control. However, once a child is conceived, new questions arise for the mother, including one very important question: *What is God's plan for this child?*

Whether they end up parenting or making an adoption plan, those brave mothers who have chosen to protect their children have found healing and consolation. Some have testified publicly about how glad they are not to have compounded their grief and pain by ending an innocent child's life—while those who have chosen abortion, often under well-meaning but misguided pressure, frequently regret their choice.[75]

St. Teresa always showed great compassion for women facing such a difficult dilemma, often with few resources and little support. To each of these women, Mother Teresa always offered the same advice: "Bring the child to me. I will take the child." One such story is found in her book *Mother Teresa's Reaching Out in Love:*

Mother Teresa frequently rescued not just unwanted infants, but their mothers as well. When the father and uncle of a young lady pressed Mother Teresa to hide her, Mother wanted to know, "Is there any love for the child?…If there is no love and the mother abandons the child, we shall give it an adoption. If there is love, the mother may call for the child after one or two years, as she likes." As the men went, relieved, Mother observed that they had saved many children that way.[76]

As Catholics, we are called to defend and protect all human life, including the unborn as well as the elderly and infirm. This tradition goes back to the first century of the Church, when Christians resisted the Roman practice of infanticide by taking into their own homes babies who had been left out in the elements to die from exposure. In contemporary times, one of the most important ways to affirm life is by helping those who are struggling to parent. One can help either informally through friendship or in a more formal way by donating to or volunteering for organizations such as crisis pregnancy centers and foster care agencies. Have you considered lending a hand?

A Moment to Reflect
- What are some of the ways the legalization of abortion has changed how our society regards marriage and family life? Why do you suppose the Church has always been firmly and unapologetically pro-life?
- What can you do to carry on the work of Mother Teresa in tending to the needs of poor mothers and their children?

A Moment to Pray
Lord, thank you for the gift of life! Show me how to do my part so that all future generations will have a voice to praise you. Help me to protect, defend, and celebrate life each and every day. St. Teresa of Calcutta, pray for us!

Wednesday of the Fifth Week of Lent
HOLY RESISTANCE
Daniel 3:14–20, 91–92, 95; Daniel 3:52, 53, 54, 55, 56; John 8:31–42

If our God whom we serve is able to deliver us from the furnace of blazing fire and out of your hand, O king, let him deliver us. But if not, be it known to you, O king, that we will not serve your gods and we will not worship the golden statue that you have set up.

—Daniel 3:17–18

In the book of Daniel, we read of the great Babylonian King Nebuchadnezzar, who holds captive at his court the young Judean prince Daniel, along with his three companions, Shadrach, Meshach, and Abednego. The young men are devout Jews, and God hears and answers their prayers in remarkable ways. In today's first reading, God spares the young men's lives after the king has them cast into a fiery furnace for refusing to bow down to his golden idol. Faced with an unjust and powerful sovereign, the faithful men turn to the Lord for deliverance, and he does not forsake them.

We see a similar dynamic of advocating for the Lord's mercy and justice with secular powers in the early religious life of Mother Teresa, who was living in Calcutta as the principal of St. Mary's School for girls during the "Great Calcutta Killings."

On August 16, 1946, riots broke out between the Hindu and Muslim factions in the city due to a combination of famine and governmental corruption. According to *Mother Teresa: A Life Inspired,* within three days more than four thousand people had been killed, their bodies piling up in the streets, and more than one hundred thousand had been left homeless. Venturing out to find rice for her students, Mother Teresa witnessed the carnage—and it was less than a month later that she heard Jesus give her the "call within a call."[77] Up until that time she had belonged to an order that served the girls from the Indian middle and upper classes; now she would be reaching out to the most needy and living among them in an unprecedented vision of missionary service.

What made the tireless efforts of St. Teresa and her Sisters most remarkable is the fact that St. Teresa was neither a cog in a political or an ecclesial institution nor, strictly speaking, part of the resistance movement for social or political change—though she recognized that things did need to be changed. Rather, her sights were firmly set on alleviating the suffering of those she and her Sisters encountered every day on the streets; the women were "warriors in saris" fighting not the institutional incompetence and corruption that produced such suffering, but the suffering itself:

> We are called to make our lives a rivalry with Christ; we are called upon to be warriors in saris, for the church needs fighters today. Our war cry has to be "fight not flight."
>
> The church of God needs saints today. We shall go freely in the name of Jesus, to towns and villages all over the world, even amid squalid and dangerous surroundings, with Mary the Immaculate Mother of Jesus, seeking out the spiritually poorest of the poor with God's own tender affection and proclaiming to them the Good News of salvation and hope, singing with them His songs, bringing to them His love, peace, and joy.[78]

What can we learn from the way of life and mission of Mother Teresa and her Sisters during that early time of tremendous political and social turmoil? First, we must take to heart her challenge to be warriors without armor, resisting the temptation to look for governmental solutions to what is at heart a personal problem and using love as a force for good in the world. Second, we must look to the Blessed Mother and imitate her maternal care in our own intercession and hidden labor. And third, we must be ready to cooperate with the Lord not just to relieve temporal suffering, but to draw those we encounter closer to God.

A Moment to Reflect

- Did you encounter any opportunities today to meet a human need by offering a personal solution to what most people consider an institutional problem?
- What is one way you can be a "warrior" in your own circle of influence in your community, parish, or neighborhood?

A Moment to Pray

Holy Spirit, in your creativity and goodness you work in the hearts that are open to your leading to bring the light of Christ even to the darkest corners of the world. Help me to shine my light a little more brightly today. St. Teresa of Calcutta, pray for us!

Thursday of the Fifth Week of Lent
WHO IS GOD?
Genesis 17:3–9; Psalm 105:4–5, 6–7, 8–9; John 8:51–59

> Then the Jews said to him, "You are not yet fifty years old, and
> have you seen Abraham?" Jesus said to them, "Very truly, I tell
> you, before Abraham was, I am."
>
> —John 8:57–58

In the first line of John's Gospel, we learn that Jesus existed as the eternal
Word long before he embraced humanity in the Incarnation: "In the
beginning was the Word, and the Word was with God, and the Word was
God" (John 1:1). Jesus's statement in today's Gospel alludes to the fact
that, as the Word, he has no beginning or end, but exists outside of the
time he created at the beginning of the world.

Back in heaven, Jesus is once again unconfined by time and space here on
earth. But he promised his disciples, "I will never leave you or forsake you"
(Hebrews 13:5), and told them, "And remember, I am with you always,
to the end of the age" (Matthew 28:20). One of the most important ways
he keeps this promise is through the mystery of his Eucharistic presence
(*CCC* 1373); one special way we acknowledge this miracle is through
spending time with Jesus in Eucharistic Adoration (*CCC* 1378–1379).

Mother Teresa found that the difficult work she and her Sisters
performed out of love for Christ was possible only if they presented themselves daily to the Lord in Adoration. She writes:

> He who spoke with authority now spends his earthly life in
> silence. Let us adore Jesus in the Eucharistic silence. We need to

find God, and he cannot be found in noise and restlessness. See how nature, the trees, the flowers and the grass grow in perfect silence. See the stars, the moon, and the sun, how they move in silence. The apostle said, "We will give ourselves continually at prayer and to the ministry of the Word." For the more we receive in silent prayer, the more we can give in our active life. We need silence to be able to touch souls. The essential thing is not what we say, but what God says to us.[79]

I've discovered through conversations with other converts to the Catholic faith that many of them identify spending time with Jesus in Eucharistic adoration as an important turning point in their journey. It was an important part of my early Catholic formation as well: sitting expectantly in front of the tabernacle, waiting for Jesus to speak to me. I always left with the strong impression that he had met me there, just as he met the friend of St. John Vianney who described his experience of Adoration very simply: "I look at Jesus, and he looks at me."[80]

This kind of stillness does not come naturally to most people. We are accustomed to rushing about, trying to get a million things done at once. Lent is the perfect time to practice the presence of God, to still our hearts and meditate on the God who wants to be near us. Listen to this reflection on who God was for Mother Teresa. Ponder each line slowly, and let the truth come alive in your heart.

God is (Exodus 3:14).
God is love (1 John 4:8).
God is everywhere (Psalm 139:7–10).
God is the Author of life (John 1:1–4).
God is a loving Father (Matthew 6:25–32).

God is a merciful Father (Tobit 13:4–6).

God is all powerful and He can take care of us (Wisdom 11:21).

God is love and God loves you and loves me (John 16:27).

God is joy (Nehemiah 8:10).

God is purity Himself.

God is with us (Matthew 1:23).

God is in love with us.

God is in your heart (Romans 10:8).

God is faithful (Deuteronomy 7:9).

God is love, God is joy, God is light, God is truth (John 8:12; 14:6).

God is thoughtful.

God is so good to us.

God is so generous.

God is so preoccupied with you.

God is a faithful lover.

God is a jealous lover (Deuteronomy 4:24).

God is so wonderful.[81]

A Moment to Reflect

- Which attribute on this list of who God was for Mother Teresa resonated with you most strongly? Would you add anything?
- When was the last time you spent some time with Jesus in Adoration? Why not make arrangements to go tomorrow?

A Moment to Pray

God, you are so wonderful. Jesus, your love is overwhelming. Thank you for waiting so patiently for me. Help me to be attentive to your holy presence in the tabernacle. St. Teresa of Calcutta, pray for us!

Friday of the Fifth Week of Lent
The Robin and the Thorn
Jeremiah 20:10–13; Psalm 18:2–3a, 3bc–4, 5–6, 7; John 10:31–42

Jesus replied, "I have shown you many good works from the Father. For which of these are you going to stone me?"

—John 10:32

It is the final Friday before Holy Week. Many parishes hold fish fries, Stations of the Cross, or penance services on this day—communal gatherings of penitential good works to finish Lent strong and prepare for Holy Week and especially the highest feast on the entire Church calendar, Easter.

If your fidelity to your Lenten intentions has gradually relaxed over the past few weeks, it is not too late to take them up with renewed vigor. If you have been steadily adhering to the disciplines and sacrifices you chose, perhaps you sometimes find yourself wondering if it really matters after all. Our good works of self-discipline are so small compared to Jesus's miracles...and compared to our failures. Can giving up chocolate or alcohol for a few weeks really make a difference in the spiritual life, when there are so many bigger fish to fry?

Does Jesus really care that I gave up chocolate...when my stress eating has me tipping the scales and dressing in muumuus?

Does he appreciate the fact I gave up my daily Diet Coke...if I get so aggravated with my kids that they hide in their rooms right after dinner?

Is he happy to see me corralling the family for vespers or Stations of the Cross…if on the car ride to the church, the air is filled with one gripe after another?

After all he did for me to reconcile my wayward heart to God, do any of these tiny, insignificant gestures do any more than add insult to injury?

I was pondering this mystery when my eye fell upon a little story in *No Greater Love* in which St. Teresa captures in a memorable way how we bring consolation to the heart of Jesus with our tiny, insignificant gestures of faith.

> There is a story of a little robin. He saw Jesus on the cross, saw the crown of thorns. The bird flew around and around until he found a way to remove a thorn, and in removing the thorn stuck himself.
>
> Each one of us should be the bird. What have I done? What comfort have I given? Does my work really mean something? The little robin tried to remove just one thorn. When I look at the cross, I think of that robin. Don't pass by the cross; it is a place of grace.[82]

Because of St. Teresa, I know that even the smallest offering of love, the tiniest good work, is returned to me mysteriously full of amazing grace. If, each time I push away my plate or can, I pause and thank the Lord for letting me take even a single thorn, then I am blessed. And if I bring my family into the church to spend a moment of silence, maybe we'll obtain for our efforts grace enough to make it through the week.

A Moment to Reflect

- What did you do today to prepare for the spiritual journey of next week?

- The Palm Sunday Gospel reading is a long one. Consider reading it with your friends or family over the next couple of days to get ready for Palm Sunday and the Triduum!

A Moment to Pray

Lord Jesus, as I approach Palm Sunday and Holy Week, help me to remain fully in the moment and to stand with you in your passion. Thank you for making a gift of yourself to me; help me to do the same for others. St. Teresa of Calcutta, pray for us!

Saturday of the Fifth Week of Lent
NEW LIFE AFTER DEATH
Ezekiel 37:21–28; Jeremiah 31:10, 11–12, 13; John 11:45–57

Many of the Jews therefore, who had come with Mary and had seen what Jesus did, believed in him. But some of them went to the Pharisees and told them what he had done.

—John 11:45–46

It is said that families are most fully themselves at funerals and weddings. At these great milestones, the relational dynamics between family members come to the foreground. For some, who recall happy memories and celebrate the life of the one who has died, even funerals can be a cause for joy, while others texture grief with additional layers of resentment or regret.

Our Christian faith can help us to navigate these challenging occasions if we willingly abandon ourselves to God, staying close to him and asking for the strength to let go of past hurts and to rise above the drama. St. Teresa of Avila said that, in addition to love, the two most important virtues of the Christian life are humility and detachment; these two virtues are especially important at the end of life, for only those who have the humility to let go of all that is not God will walk the way of the saints.

Because she spent so much time with the dying, Mother Teresa understood the significance of the final moments before death; she attended to each dying soul the way a doula attends a woman in labor, helping the person focus on what was most important: the new life that is just in sight. The saint understood that forgiveness was often the key to a peaceful death. On one occasion, she attended a woman who was angry with her son for abandoning her, leaving her to die on a garbage heap.

> This woman was so hurt that her own child didn't want her; her son whom she had borne. She had given him love and care and now he had no use for her. I begged her to forgive her son, to be a mother to her son. After a long time, she whispered in her last breath, "I forgive him, my God, I forgive him."[83]

In today's Gospel, we read about the fallout from the miracle Jesus performed in raising his friend, Lazarus, from the dead. As might be expected, Jesus won many followers that day, people who were amazed that this prophet had the power to restore a dead man to life. Yet others reacted with suspicion and fear and cast their lot with the religious authorities of the day rather than open their eyes to believe in the resurrecting power of God.

As we head into Holy Week, we return to the predominant theme of the Gospel message: dying and rising to new life. St. Paul said it best: "If we live, we live to the Lord, and if we die, we die to the Lord; so then, whether we live or whether we die, we are the Lord's" (Romans 14:8) and "For to me, living is Christ and dying is gain" (Philippians 1:21). Each moment we practice virtue (live to the Lord) and detach from selfishness and pride (die to the Lord), we embrace more fully God's plan for our lives and become more fully who God created us to be—and who we will be for all eternity. Let us believe and keep our eyes on eternity.

A Moment to Reflect

- As you look back on your life, does your mind go to a particular person you need to forgive or a particular memory you need to let go of in order to experience peace?

- Tomorrow is Palm Sunday, the first day of Holy Week, when we hear the story of the passion and the final days of the life of Christ. Are you ready to put yourself in the story?

A Moment to Pray

Jesus, you raised your friend Lazarus from the grave, knowing that you would soon be giving your life for his. Help me show that kind of self-sacrificing love, so that my life will be full of forgiveness and peace. St. Teresa of Calcutta, pray for us!

Holy Week
STANDING WITH CHRIST IN HIS PASSION

Palm Sunday of the Lord's Passion
I HAVE DECIDED TO FOLLOW JESUS

Procession Gospel: Year A: Matthew 21:1–11; Year B: Mark 11:1–10 or John 12:12–16; Year C: Luke 19:28–40

First Reading, Psalm, Second Reading: Year A, B, C: Isaiah 50:4–7; Psalm 22:8–9, 17–18, 19–20, 23–24; Philippians 2:6–11

Gospel: Year A: Matthew 26:14—27:66; Year B: Mark 14:1—15:47; Year C: Luke 22:14—23:56

As he was now approaching the path down from the Mount of Olives, the whole multitude of the disciples began to praise God joyfully with a loud voice for all the deeds of power that they had seen, saying,
"Blessed is the king
who comes in the name of the Lord! Peace in heaven,
and glory in the highest heaven!"

—Luke 19:37–38

The final week of Lent is the prelude to Easter, the highest and greatest feast of the entire Church year. From the jubilant moment Jesus enters Jerusalem as a king on the back of that colt, to the shameful moment he shoulders his own cross to walk the Via Dolorosa, to the sorrowful moment he is laid in the borrowed tomb of Joseph of Arimathea, the symphony of the passion story builds to the crescendo of the resurrection—when once and for all the Risen Lord shatters the bonds of sin and death, leading us forth to glory.

Each year we follow this familiar path in liturgy and ritual, and yet if it never becomes more than ritual—if those palm fronds are nothing more than a religious accessory to be saved for their ashes the following Lent—we entirely miss the point. We are meant to follow Jesus through death to resurrection. "The saying is sure," writes the apostle Paul to his spiritual son, Timothy, "If we have died with him, we will also live with him;/ if we endure, we will also reign with him;/ if we deny him, he will also deny us;/ if we are faithless, he remains faithful—for he cannot deny himself" (2 Timothy 2:11–13).

So just how closely will we follow Jesus, our king? Once the cheers of the crowd have died down and we have placed our palms back up on the bookshelf, what next? Will we betray the Lord with our words and actions, as Judas did (see Matthew 26:47–50)? Will we fall asleep, as did the disciples with Jesus in the garden (see Matthew 26:40), or deny that we know him at all (Matthew 26:69–74)? Or will we follow him all the way to Golgotha—even if it means taking up our own cross—so that we experience the joy of Easter?

Listen to the words of Mother Teresa:

Our thoughts turn to the passion and death of our Lord, and we long to share his pain with him. What is the pain of Jesus? It is the pain of loving and not being loved in return. He has loved us with an everlasting love, and what do we give him in return? We allow our minds to be preoccupied with little things and so spend many hours without thinking of Jesus. And yet our hearts and minds, bodies and souls, belong only to him.

Let us meditate on the sufferings of Christ each day. We often pray, "Jesus, let me share in your pain." Yet when a thorn of thoughtlessness comes our way or a little spittle in the form of an uncharitable remark, we forget that this is the time to share with him his shame and his pain.[84]

Imagine, then, that you are on the road into Jerusalem Hear the pandemonium of the crowd, so enthralled and full of messianic hope. Are you cheering along or looking fearfully about, wondering if the Roman soldiers will catch wind of the gathering and rush in to break up the demonstration? Are you energized by the celebration, or are you more conscious of your weary arms and legs? Can you see the face of Jesus, calmly accepting the adulation of the crowd, knowing it will not last? And when at last he looks at you…what do you wish to say to him?

Jesus, let me stay with you. Let me share in your pain.

In the end, we can only follow at a distance, limited by the bounds of space and time. And yet we can also, as Mother Teresa reminds us, share his pain in a small way with countless small acts of love, each done in recognition of "Jesus in distressing disguise."

Where will you begin today?

A Moment to Reflect

- Today's Gospel, which is proclaimed as a dramatic reading in many parishes, captures the drama of the passion in its entirety. What part of the reading spoke most powerfully to you today?
- Which of the Holy Week liturgies do you plan to attend this week? Take a moment to look in today's bulletin, and mark your calendar. Make it your intention to follow Jesus as closely as possible during Holy Week.

A Moment to Pray

Hosanna, Lord Jesus! You are my king, my master, my savior. Help me to follow you as closely as did your beloved disciple during Holy Week. Give me strength to take up my own cross and follow you, wherever you choose to lead me. St. Teresa of Calcutta, pray for us!

Monday of Holy Week
THE OTHER MARY'S MOMENT
Isaiah 42:1–7; Psalm 27:1, 2, 3, 13–14; John 12:1–11

Mary took a pound of costly perfume made of pure nard, anointed Jesus' feet, and wiped them with her hair. The house was filled with the fragrance of the perfume.

—John 12:3

The story of the woman who anoints the feet of Jesus—and is roundly criticized for her act of devotion—can be found in all four Gospels.[85] While Matthew and Mark are ambiguous about the identity of the woman, choosing instead to focus on the location of the event (at Simon's house), Luke and John add identifying details. Luke describes her as "a woman in the city, who was a sinner" (7:37), while the beloved disciple says it was Mary of Bethany (the sister of Lazarus) who anointed Jesus while her sister Martha served the meal (John 12:2–3).

In a sense, it is no wonder that the other two apostles are reluctant to say much about the woman who performs this intimate ritual for Jesus. Setting aside all propriety, she uncovers both her head and his feet in full view of all those present, touching and kissing him, and then wiping her "glory"[86] on the lowest part of his body. In purely human terms, she is debasing herself and destroying her own reputation; in the sight of God, she is uniquely and sacrificially preparing Jesus to fulfill his destiny. At a time when everyone around him seems to be pressing him to do more and give more, she alone sees him fully, in all his human need, and does what she can to strengthen him.

The Scriptures do not tell us whether the Blessed Mother was present. It seems likely that she would have traveled with Jesus to see his friends, though perhaps she was back in the kitchen with Martha and the other women. But if she witnessed the anointing, surely she looked into that young woman's eyes and saw the love, and looked into her Son's and saw the gratitude. And perhaps, in guiding Martha's sister safely back to the private quarters, Jesus's mother would have found herself strangely comforted as well.

Meditating on the events of Holy Week, I often think about the Blessed Mother and what she did and thought as she witnessed the final week of her Son's life. For Mother Teresa, staying close to Mary was "a woman's way to the heart of Christ."[87] And so we can offer up this prayer with St. Teresa:

> O most pure heart of Mary, allow me to enter your heart, to share your interior life. You see and know my needs; help me to "do whatever Jesus tells me"…that my human needs be changed into thirst for God alone.[88]

A Moment to Reflect

- When you read this Gospel story, try to put yourself in the picture. See the woman breaking open the precious jar, and smell the aroma of the oil. Hear the critical words of Judas and the reproachful ones of Jesus. Stand beside Mary, and watch and pray.

- The temptation of Holy Week is to "race for the cross," to keep our eyes so focused on the crucifixion that we miss the signs of hope and promise leading up to that gruesome event. Make sure to listen to the cries of the crowd who welcome their king entering the city on a donkey. Taste the wine of the Last Supper. Hear the dying confession of the good thief. Stay awake. Remain vigilant. God is near.

A Moment to Pray

Blessed Mother, no doubt you were startled at Mary's actions as she began to anoint your Son's feet and pondered the meaning of this strange event. Let me stay with you and ponder, too. St. Teresa of Calcutta, pray for us!

Tuesday of Holy Week
LORD, WHO IS IT?
Isaiah 49:1–6; Psalm 71:1–2, 3–4a, 5–6ab, 15, 17; John 13:21–33, 36–38

After saying this Jesus was troubled in spirit, and declared, "Very truly, I tell you, one of you will betray me." The disciples looked at one another, uncertain of whom he was speaking. One of his disciples—the one whom Jesus loved—was reclining next to him; Simon Peter therefore motioned to him to ask Jesus of whom he was speaking. So while reclining next to Jesus, he asked him, "Lord, who is it?"

—John 13:21–25

Other than the facts that he carried the money for the group and betrayed Christ, we know relatively little about Judas Iscariot. Scripture does not record what he did before he became an apostle or how he came to follow Jesus. Even in his duties as treasurer, Judas's motives are questioned by the other apostles (John 12:4–6). Yet he remains there on the periphery, watchful. Perhaps, like Judas Maccabeus, Iscariot was a warrior at heart, waiting for the Messiah who would defeat the hated Romans. And perhaps this is why "Satan entered into Judas called Iscariot" (Luke 22:3) not long after Jesus predicted the destruction of Jerusalem (see Luke 21:20–24).

It's hard to get a read on the relationship between Jesus and this follower, the very sight of whom must have been a painful reminder to Jesus of what was in store for him. And yet, as Mother Teresa points out, we can learn a great deal from the way Jesus treated Judas. In particular, we see what it is to love someone who refuses to love you back.

When Judas came to betray Him…"Friend, will you betray Me with a kiss?", He never said, "You traitor."[89] Same at the washing of the feet—though there was agony in His heart…He was never harsh. Again while hanging on the cross, looking at His mother, looking at St. John, He thought of us. Who will take care of my mother? Who will take care of John? Whenever someone corrects you, scolds you, instead of becoming bitter, think of Jesus, how He thought of others even in His agony and pain. Never allow bitterness to remain in your heart.

Very often I think of Jesus—from the beginning He knew Judas would betray him. For three years Jesus knew, and even at the end, when [Judas] came to destroy Him, Jesus didn't call him a traitor, He didn't push him away, but called him "friend." Wonderful, wonderful example of Jesus' tender love. [90]

How often do we, because of our own agendas and priorities, betray the name of Jesus or use our relationship with him to our own advantage? How often do we look to gain advantage over another soul, equally beloved of God, in our prayers and in how we relate to other Christians? How often do we cooperate with evil by committing slander or gossip or anger or pride or unforgiveness, and how often do we expect God to look the other way? Is this not also a betrayal of the Lord?

"Lord, who is it?" In the end, Judas destroyed himself by his refusal to repent, while Peter repented and was reconciled with Christ. We need to take these words of the beloved disciple to heart before we receive the Lord in his Eucharistic presence. Make things right with God, so the next time you receive the bread, you won't hear Jesus say to you, "Do quickly what you are going to do" (John 13:27).

A Moment to Reflect

- Have you betrayed the Lord today? Will you take advantage of his patient love, as Judas did, or be reconciled with him, as Peter did?
- How can you extend the forgiveness and love of Jesus to someone who has betrayed or taken advantage of you in the past?

A Moment to Pray

Forgive me, Jesus, for not taking seriously all the little ways that I betray your love and ignore your pain. Help me to forgive as I want to be forgiven. St. Teresa of Calcutta, pray for us!

Wednesday of Holy Week
MAKE SOMETHING BEAUTIFUL

Isaiah 50:4–9a; Psalm 69:8–10, 21–22, 31, 33–34; Matthew 26:14–25

[Jesus] said, "Go into the city to a certain man, and say to him, 'The Teacher says, My time is near; I will keep the Passover at your house with my disciples.'" So the disciples did as Jesus had directed them, and they prepared the Passover meal.

—Matthew 26:18–19

One of the advantages of working from home is that my life has greater fluidity than it would if I went an office every day. In the same amount of time it used to take me to drive to work, I can assemble dinner in the slow cooker, or rotate the laundry, or drive a child to an appointment. It's a great gift, though the challenges of finding a good work-life balance are still there.

As the "keeper of beauty" in our home, I often wonder if I'm making the most of the little celebrations and other memorable events that are the heartbeat of family life. Sure, I can whip together a dinner in fifteen minutes…but how many of these will be memorable meals? When the family gathers to play a board game with popcorn, I think about the lack of creativity of this pastime compared to the cleverness of moms who create Mary gardens and Jesse trees and homemade quilts out of old t-shirts. As Easter draws closer, I contemplate making with my children the special bread with the colored eggs—a loaf for us and another to give away—and wonder if this is the kind of memory that will stay with them.

In his famous biography of Mother Teresa, *Something Beautiful for God*, Malcolm Muggeridge summarizes her life and work in a way that encourages me as a busy mom. I want to share it with you, too, in the hope that it will inspire you to go out and "make something beautiful for God," as she did.

> Doing something beautiful for God is, for Mother Teresa, what life is about. Everything, in that it is for God, becomes beautiful, whatever it may be; as does every human soul participating in this purpose, whoever he or she may be. In manifesting this, in themselves and in their lives and work, Mother Teresa and the Missionaries of Charity provide a living witness to the power and truth of what Jesus came to proclaim. His light shines in them. When I think of them in Calcutta, as I often do, it is not the bare house in a dark slum that is conjured up in my mind, but a light shining and a joy abounding. I see them diligently and cheerfully constructing something beautiful for God out of the human misery and affliction that lies around them.[91]

In today's Gospel, the disciples of Jesus are sent on a most practical mission, to prepare the room (known as the Upper Room or Cenacle) in which Jesus and the apostles will celebrate the Feast of Unleavened Bread (Passover). This is the festival at which Jews remember their deliverance from slavery in Egypt. It must have seemed like a trivial chore at the time, to find the room and make it ready for the feast. Had the disciples been at home, much of the preparation would normally have fallen to their wives or to servants. But this year, as they carried out Jesus's enigmatic instructions, they had a strong sense of purpose. And then, as the evening began…they discovered it was to be no ordinary Pesach.

Without knowing it, that day they had done something beautiful for God.

A Moment to Reflect

- Looking back on your day, can you identify any action that seemed like a waste of time in the moment, but was actually an opportunity to do "something beautiful for God"?
- Tomorrow begins the Triduum, the high holy days of the Easter season. Mother Teresa said that "holiness is one of the most important gifts a human heart can offer to God."[92] What can you do to grow in holiness between now and Easter?

A Moment to Pray

Holy Spirit, enter the cenacle of my heart and sweep it clean. Make me ready to receive the Body of Christ, in his resurrected glory. St. Teresa of Calcutta, pray for us!

The Easter Triduum: Holy Thursday
IN THE CENACLE
Exodus 12:1–8, 11–14; Psalm 116:12–13, 15–16, 17–18;
1 Corinthians 11:23–26; John 13:1–5

And during supper Jesus, knowing that the Father had given all things into his hands, and that he had come from God and was going to God, got up from the table, took off his outer robe, and tied a towel around himself.

—John 13:2b–4

In *Meeting God in the Upper Room,* Monsignor Peter Vaghi identifies three important "moments" in Christian history that transpired in the Cenacle in Jerusalem. The event most people associate with the Cenacle is the Last Supper, in which Jesus institutes the Eucharist. Monsignor Vaghi also speaks of the post-resurrection appearances of Christ and of Pentecost, showing how these events prepared the apostles to follow Jesus on a mission of lifelong service.

This twofold mission of communion and service is also at the heart of the work of the Missionaries of Charity. For St. Teresa, the Eucharist and the work of religious life were inextricably intertwined:

The Eucharist is connected with the Passion. If Jesus had not established the Eucharist, we would have forgotten the crucifixion. It would have faded into the past and we would have forgotten that Jesus loved us. There is a saying that to be far away from the eyes is to be far away from the heart. To make sure that we do not forget, Jesus gave us the Eucharist as a memorial of his love. To make sure that we keep on loving him, he gives us his hunger (to satisfy our hunger for him)—he gives us the poorest of the poor.

We must be faithful to that smallness of the Eucharist, that simple piece of bread which even a child can take in, that giving of a bath, that smile.… We have so much that we don't care about the small things. If we do not care, we will lose our grip on the Eucharist—on our lives. The Eucharist is so small.[93]

In emphasizing the smallness of the Eucharist, Mother Teresa was of course not diminishing its importance in our lives. Rather, she was emphasizing the gentleness and meekness of Jesus, who condescends to wait patiently for us in the tabernacle, or at Mass, or in the sacrament of reconciliation. Though he remains the Prince of Peace, seated at the right hand of God the Father, he does not demand our fealty or devotion. Instead, he waits… dressed as a servant ready to wash us clean or feed our souls; or hidden in the guise of a piece of bread, listening to hear our innermost prayers.

And so today, as you watch the familiar foot-washing ritual with the priest taking the place of Christ, enter fully into that moment in sacred history. Imagine what was going through the minds of the disciples as their feet were washed, the cup of wine was blessed, and the Lord spoke those momentous words to all present: "Take, eat; this is my body…" Receive the Lord as though it were your first time as well.

A Moment to Reflect

- The Eucharist was such a central part of Mother Teresa's spirituality that she was certain we would have forgotten about Christ's crucifixion if he had not given us the Eucharist. Do you agree?

- If possible, spend some time in prayer for those who are contemplating a priestly vocation or a call to religious life. Do you know anyone currently contemplating this step who could use a word of encouragement?

A Moment to Pray

Lord Jesus, in your humility and love you spent your last few hours on earth teaching your disciples what it means to lead through service and strengthening them to do this important work by offering them yourself. Thank you, Lord, for holy priests and religious. Help me to offer myself in loving service according to the vocation you have given me. St. Teresa of Calcutta, pray for us!

The Easter Triduum: Good Friday
AT THE FOOT OF THE CROSS

Isaiah 52:13—53:12; Psalm 31:2, 6, 12–13, 15–16, 17, 25;
Hebrews 4:14–16; 5:7–9; John 18:1—19:42

One of the soldiers pierced his side with a spear, and at once
blood and water came out.

—John 19:34

The torturous ordeal that Jesus endured, from the moment he was taken
prisoner in the Garden of Gethsemane until he was laid to rest in the tomb
of Joseph of Arimathea, is captured through a series of fourteen images
known as the Stations of the Cross. Although the events depicted in the
devotion have changed only slightly since the Franciscans began building
outdoor shrines for spiritual pilgrimages from the mid-fifteenth century,
Pope John Paul II introduced a new "Scriptural Way of the Cross" on
Good Friday, 1991:
- Jesus in the Garden of Gethsemane (Matthew 26:36)
- Jesus is betrayed by Judas and arrested (Matthew 26:50)
- Jesus is condemned by the Sanhedrin (Matthew 26:66)
- Jesus is denied by Peter (Matthew 26:72)
- Jesus is judged by Pilate (Matthew 27:1)
- Jesus is scourged and crowned with thorns (Matthew 27:29)
- Jesus takes up his cross (John 19:17)
- Jesus is helped by Simon of Cyrene to carry his cross (Matthew 27:32)
- Jesus meets the women of Jerusalem (Luke 23:28)

- Jesus is crucified (Matthew 27:35)
- Jesus promises his kingdom to the repentant thief (Luke 23:43)
- Jesus entrusts Mary and John to each other (John 19:26–27)
- Jesus dies on the cross (Matthew 27:50)
- Jesus is laid in the tomb (Matthew 27:59)

These scriptural stations are a wonderful guide to meditating on Christ's passion if you are unable to attend the Holy Week liturgies today. The traditional stations can be found either in the sanctuary or on the grounds of many parishes, and taking time to walk them and reflect upon the story of the passion can be a wonderful way to remind yourself of and introduce children to the story of Jesus and his love for us.

For Mother Teresa, the story of the passion of the Lord was closely connected to that of the Blessed Mother, who followed her Son every step of the way, not sparing herself even a moment of his agony.

> With the crowd [Our Lady] also moves toward Calvary. She meets Jesus on the way, face to face. She must have seen his body beaten, full of wounds, the head from the crowning [with thorns] bleeding, face dirty with spittle and swollen with blows, hands full of blood. What a sight! What she must have felt. She had the courage to look at her Son and suffer with Him. We don't hear her voice. She followed Jesus until the Cross—the selfless love of a mother. She stood by [Him] in His humiliations, up to the Cross. She must have heard the people speaking badly about Him, the High Priest, the Pharisees and the others, cursing and saying ugly things. Her silence was great; she knew who her Son was. She didn't fall on the ground, didn't try to catch attention

on herself. She stood by the Cross…. The true love of the mother is shown when her children suffer.[94]

Reading this final line, I am moved to think about the spiritual motherhood of St. Teresa, who must have suffered terribly because she was able to do so little to alleviate the suffering of so many of her poor "children." When our children suffer, they need us to stay near, to comfort them in their pain. And so, when we stay with Jesus on Good Friday, lingering in prayer after the liturgy is over to remember what he suffered for us, is it possible that we by our very presence sustain our Savior in his suffering?

A Moment to Reflect

- As you walked or meditated upon the stations, at which one of them were you most compelled to linger? What makes you connect with that station in such a personal way?
- As Jesus is taken down from his cross and placed in the tomb, we have the historical advantage over his grieving disciples: we know that without Good Friday, there can be no Easter Sunday, and that the resurrection surely follows the crucifixion. And so we wait. What will you do with this waiting time?

A Moment to Pray

Lord Jesus, what depths of love and mercy kept you nailed to that cross, bleeding out your life for me! In your agony, you poured out your love for your mother and disciples and did not strike back at the injustice of it all. O Lord, I cannot grasp so great a love! St. Teresa of Calcutta, pray for us!

The Easter Triduum: Holy Saturday / Easter Vigil
SEA OF MERCY

The Liturgy of the Word at the Easter Vigil includes seven readings from
the Old Testament, with psalm responses; Exodus 14:15—15:1 must always
be used; Romans 6:3—11; Psalm 118:1–2, 16–17, 22–23
Gospel: Year A: Matthew 28:1–10; Year B: Mark 16:1–7;
Year C: Luke 24:1–12

> Then Moses stretched out his hand over the sea. The Lord drove
> the sea back by a strong east wind all night, and turned the sea
> into dry land; and the waters were divided. The Israelites went
> into the sea on dry ground, the waters forming a wall for them
> on their right and on their left.
>
> —Exodus 14:21–22

In this story from the book of Exodus, Moses miraculously parts the Red
Sea so his people can escape the soldiers of Pharaoh and make their way
to freedom. According to tradition, this miracle is a sign of the sacrament
of baptism, but what the story reminds me of is standing outside the front
doors of Holy Family parish at the Easter Vigil of 1994, waiting along
with the rest of my RCIA class to be admitted into full communion with
the Catholic Church. In my hand was the candle that had been lit from
the Easter fire, and over my shoulder hung a red sash, indicating that
I was a candidate (that is, I had already been baptized). As those heavy
wooden doors ahead of me were pushed open and I ventured inside, I felt
for all the world as though I were being swallowed up. On my left and
right, from the stained glass and statuary, holy men and women watched

solemnly as I made my way to the front. I was keenly aware of what I was leaving behind, having already had several friends and at least one family member try to talk me out of taking this step.

And yet, there I was. I felt alone and overwhelmed, but I knew there was no going back. I had spent the entire day in retreat with the others in my group; a good part of that time found me sitting silently in the presence of the Lord in the tabernacle, feeling that unmistakable undercurrent of peace I had felt there so many times before. There was no telling what was ahead, but that didn't matter. God spoke to me in that silence.

"In the silence of the heart, God speaks," St. Teresa affirms, for all of us. When our doubts build up like a tsunami, or our love begins to fail and weakness besets us and lays us low, we can always meet the Lord in the silence of our hearts.

> In the silence of the heart, God speaks. If you face God in prayer and silence, God will speak to you. Then you will know that you are nothing. It is only when you realize your nothingness, your emptiness, that God can fill you with himself. Souls of prayer are souls of great silence.
>
> There is a very holy priest, who is also one of the best theologians in India right now.... I said to him, "Father, you talk all day about God. How close you must be to God!" And do you know what he said to me? He said, "I may be talking much *about* God, but I may be talking very little *to* God.... I may be rattling off so many words and may be saying many good things, but deep down I do not have the time to listen. Because in the silence of the heart, God speaks."[95]

There was a time when I believed that I was a failure as a Christian if I didn't have just the right Bible verse at the tip of my tongue, or know exactly the right prayer to offer in any desperate situation, or present an iron-clad response to any theological or spiritual objection someone might make about what I believe. As a Catholic, I have come to appreciate that God loves a humble heart and gives wisdom to those who urgently seek it.

And so, looking up at Monsignor Connelly, the dear Irish priest who had so patiently answered my many questions, and seeing the glint of joy in his eye as he held up the host and murmured "The Body of Christ" to me, I was glad there was only one word I needed to say at that moment.

"Amen."

A Moment to Reflect

- Did you have a chance to attend the Vigil Mass at your parish and welcome the new Catholics who were confirmed this year? Take a moment to pray for them, that God continue to help them grow in faith in the coming year.
- Alleluia! It's time to rejoice in the Risen Lord! How will you celebrate Easter in a way that renews your faith—and maybe even someone else's?

A Moment to Pray

Risen Lord, you are my joy, my strength, and my hope. In joy and in sorrow, in silence or jubilance, you are my heart's great desire. St. Teresa of Calcutta, pray for us!

Easter Triduum: Easter Sunday
Help Me to Spread Your Fragrance

Acts 10:34a, 37–43; Psalm 118:1–2, 16–17, 22–23; Colossians 3:1–4 or 1 Corinthians 5:6b–8; John 20:1–9

> Early on the first day of the week, while it was still dark, Mary Magdalene came to the tomb and saw that the stone had been removed from the tomb.
>
> —John 20:1

Although all four Gospels speak of the resurrection of the Lord, each narrative captures different details. We learn in John's account that the Lord's body is anointed by Joseph of Arimathea and Nicodemus (19:38–40). The Franciscans who are the caretakers of the site believed to be the tomb of Jesus offer this historical context:

> In this fourth Gospel, the only one that makes reference to Nicodemus, John mentions an exorbitant mixture of one hundred (Roman) pounds—about 33 kilograms—composed of myrrh, an aromatic resin, and aloe, a perfume, undoubtedly with the aim of showing that the dead person was truly king, as had been written on the tablet attached to the Cross, and as he had been treated.[96]

John also records that after the Sabbath, Mary Magdalene goes to the tomb and sees that the stone has been rolled away; she rushes to find Peter and John: "They have taken the Lord out of the tomb, and we do not know where they have laid him" (20:2).

Matthew recalls that the men guarding the tomb see the angel and fall over like dead men in terror (28:4). Luke claims that the disciples do not initially believe the women until they see the empty tomb for themselves (24:11).

The normally taciturn Mark, who, according to tradition, relies on Peter's account, recalls that Mary goes to the tomb with other women in order to anoint Jesus's body with spices—but the women scatter in terror when they encounter an angel outside the tomb (16:1–8). This image of women carrying spices for Jesus and scattering with them is a beautiful metaphor for the life and work of Mother Teresa, who said: "Jesus is the Life that I want to live."[97]

One of the ways she and her Sisters have carried out this mission of devotion is through daily prayer. Each morning, wherever they are in the world, the Missionaries of Charity raise their voices to declare their intention to be the fragrance of Jesus in the world, using the words of Blessed John Henry Newman.

> Dear Lord:
>
> Help me to spread your fragrance wherever I go.
>
> Flood my soul with your spirit and life.
>
> Penetrate and possess my whole being so utterly that all my life may only be a radiance of yours.
>
> Shine through me, and be so in me that every soul I come in contact with may feel your presence in my soul.
>
> Let them look up and see no longer me, but only you, O Lord!
>
> Stay with me, then I shall begin to shine as you do, to shine as to be a light to others.

The light, O Lord, will be all from you; none of it will be mine; it will be you shining on others through me.

Let me thus praise you in the way you love best, by shining on those around me.

Let me preach you without preaching, not by words but by my example, by the catching force, the sympathetic influence of what I do, the evident fullness of the love my heart bears to you.

Amen.[98]

A Moment to Reflect

- Think about the signs of Easter you encountered today. Which are the most important? How can you sustain this sense of resurrection in your life?
- St. Teresa and her Missionaries of Charity have made it their life's work to spread the fragrance of Jesus wherever they go, challenging us to do the same. What is one way you can do this in the coming week?

A Moment to Pray

Risen Lord, fill my heart with your Easter presence, so that everyone I encounter will see you in me. Help me, like Mary Magdalene and the apostles, to receive the news of your resurrected life with such overwhelming joy that I can't help but share it with others.

St. Teresa of Calcutta, thank you for your witness to the world through your life, your words, and the continuing work of your Sisters. St. Teresa of Calcutta, pray for us!

Notes

1. Gerard O'Connell, "Pope Says Nuns Killed in Yemen Are Victims of 'the Globalization of Indifference,'" *America*, March 6, 2016, http://americamagazine.org/content/dispatches/pope-says-four-nuns-were-killed-yemen-their-attackers-and-globalization.

2. "Four Nuns of Mother Teresa Slain by Gunmen in Yemen," Vatican Radio website, April 3, 2016, http://en.radiovaticana.va/news/2016/03/04/four_nuns_of_mother_teresa_slain_by_gunmen_in_yemen/1213055.

3. Joan Frawley Desmond, "Eyewitness Account of ISIS Attack on Mother Teresa's Sisters in Yemen," *National Catholic Register,* March 17, 2016, http://www.ncregister.com/daily-news/eyewitness-account-of-isis-attack-on-mother-teresas-sisters-in-yemen/.

4. Sr. Rio and Sr. Adriana, handwritten account, 1, http://www.newadvent.org/library/sister-rio.pdf.

5. Sr. Rio and Sr. Adriana, 3.

6. Lauretta Brown, "Nun Gives Eyewitness Account of Islamic State's Murder of 4 Missionaries of Charity in Yemen," CNSNews.com, March 18, 2016, http://cnsnews.com/news/article/lauretta-brown/surviving-nun-gives-chilling-eyewitness-account-isis-murder-4-catholic.

7. Sr. Rio and Sr. Adriana, 2.

8. As quoted in Mother Teresa, *No Greater Love,* comp. LaVonne Neff (Novato, CA: New World Library, 2002), 158.

9. An exception to this is the Feast of St. Joseph, which is typically celebrated on March 19 unless that date happens to fall on a Sunday, in which case the feast is moved to the following Monday. This book's meditation on St. Joseph appears on the Monday of the third week of Lent.

10. Kerri Lenartowick, "Pope Francis: Be Courageous, Go to Confession," Catholic News Agency, February 19, 2014, http://www.catholicnewsagency.com/news/pope-be-courageous-go-to-confession/.

11. David Scott, *A Revolution of Love: The Meaning of Mother Teresa* (Chicago: Loyola, 2005), 24.

12. Adapted from Mother Teresa, *Thirsting for God: Daily Meditations,* ed. Angelo D. Scolozzi (Cincinnati: Servant, 2013), 21.

13. Scott, 14.
14. Adapted from Mother Teresa, *One Heart Full of Love,* ed. José Luis González-Balado (Cincinnati: Servant, 1988), 8.
15. Mother Teresa, *Thirsting for God,* 112.
16. Malcolm Muggeridge, *Something Beautiful for God* (San Francisco: Harper&Row, 1971), 22.
17. For information about volunteer opportunities with the Missionaries of Charity in Calcutta and in other parts of the world, go to http://www.motherteresa.org/07_family/volunteering/v_cal.html.
18. Mother Teresa, *Total Surrender,* ed. Angelo Devananda Scolozzi (Cincinnati: St. Anthony Messenger, 1985), 99.
19. Francis de Sales, *Introduction to the Devout Life* (1619), 31, http://www.catholicspiritualdirection.org/devoutlife.pdf.
20. According to the study notes for this passage in *The Catholic Study Bible,* 3rd ed. (New York: Oxford University Press, 2016), 764, this psalm, "a lament, the most famous of the seven Penitential Psalms, prays for the removal of the personal and social disorders that sin has brought."
21. Mother Teresa, *A Simple Path,* comp. Lucinda Vardey (New York: Ballantine Books, 1995), Kindle edition, 7.
22. Adapted from Kim Boyce and Heidi Hess Saxton, *Touched by Kindness* (Ann Arbor, MI: Vine, 2001), 67–68.
23. Mother Teresa, "The Greatest Destroyer of Peace is Abortion" in *Speeches of Mother Teresa and Other Women Leaders,* ed. Ritu Chauhan (New Delhi: Mind Melodies, 2011), 7.
24. *Mother Teresa's Reaching Out in Love: Stories Told by Mother Teresa,* ed. Edward Le Joly and Jaya Chaliha (New York: Barnes & Noble, 2002), 44–45.
25. Mother Teresa, *Thirsting for God,* 104.
26. Mother Teresa, *One Heart Full of Love,* 15.
27. Mother Teresa, *One Heart Full of Love,* 27.
28. *Mother Teresa: In My Own Words,* ed. José Luis González-Balado (Liguori, MO: Liguori, 1989), 37.
29. Mother Teresa, *One Heart Full of Love,* 28.
30. Mother Teresa, *Thirsting for God,* 143.
31. Paul Murray, *I Loved Jesus in the Night* (Brewster, MA: Paraclete, 2008), 18.
32. James Martin, "A Saint's Dark Night," *New York Times,* August 29, 2007, http://www.nytimes.com/2007/08/29/opinion/29martin.html?_r=0.

33. *Mother Teresa's Reaching Out in Love,* 86.
34. Navin Chawla, *Mother Teresa: The Authorized Biography* (Rockport, MA: Element, 1992), 186.
35. *Mother Teresa's Reaching Out in Love,* 86.
36. Filip Mazurczak, "The Scandal of Mother Teresa," *The Catholic Thing,* January 9, 2016, https://www.thecatholicthing.org/2016/01/09/ the-scandal-of-mother-teresa/.
37. Navin B. Chawla, "The Mother Teresa Her Critics Choose to Ignore," *The Hindu,* August 26, 2013, http://www.thehindu.com/opinion/lead/the-mother-teresa-her-critics-choose-to-ignore/article5058894.ece.
38. John Paul II, "Message of His Holiness John Paul II for Lent 1993," September 18, 1992, http://w2.vatican.va/content/john-paul-ii/en/messages/lent/documents/hf_jp-ii_mes_19091992_lent-1993.html.
39. Mother Teresa, *Mother Teresa: Come Be My Light—The Private Writings of the Saint of Calcutta,* ed. Brian Kolodiejchuk (New York: Doubleday, 2009), 319.
40. Mother Teresa, *Thirsting for God,* 47.
41. See Deuteronomy 22:20–21.
42. See Matthew 1:18–19.
43. Mother Teresa, *Where There Is Love, There Is God: A Path to Closer Union with God and Greater Love for Others,* ed. Brian Kolodiejchuk (New York: Crown, 2010), Kindle edition, 42–43.
44. Mother Teresa, *One Heart Full of Love,* 111–112.
45. Mother Teresa, *One Heart Full of Love,* 113.
46. *Mother Teresa's Reaching Out in Love,* 56.
47. *Mother Teresa's Reaching Out in Love,* 115.
48. Mother Teresa, *Total Surrender,* 71–72.
49. Donna-Marie Cooper O'Boyle, *Bringing Lent Home with Mother Teresa* (South Bend, IN: Ave Maria, 2012), Friday, Third Week of Lent.
50. Cooper O'Boyle, Friday, Third Week of Lent.
51. Scott, 64.
52. Desmond Doig, *Mother Teresa: Her People and Her Work* (New York: Nachiketa, 1976), 159.
53. *Mother Teresa's Reaching Out in Love,* 100.
54. *Mother Teresa's Reaching Out in Love,* 80.

55. Mother Teresa, *Thirsting for God*, 90.
56. Mother Teresa, *A Simple Path*, 89.
57. Eileen Egan and Kathleen Egan, OSB, *Suffering into Joy: What Mother Teresa Teaches about True Joy* (Ann Arbor, MI: Servant, 1994), 81.
58. *Mother Teresa's Reaching Out in Love,* 96.
59. Mother Teresa, *Thirsting for God*, 95.
60. Egan and Egan, 35.
61. Susan Conroy, *Mother Teresa's Lessons of Love and Secrets of Sanctity* (Huntington, IN: Our Sunday Visitor, 2003), 143.
62. Mother Teresa, *Come Be My Light*, 98.
63. Mother Teresa, *Come Be My Light*, 42.
64. *The Catholic Study Bible*, 123: "It seems that the golden calf was intended as an image, not of another god, but of the Lord, whose strength was symbolized by the strength of a young bull. The Israelites, however, had been forbidden to represent the Lord under any visible form, Cf. 20:4."
65. Mother Teresa, *Total Surrender,* 38.
66. Mother Teresa, *A Simple Path*, 94.
67. *Mother Teresa: In My Own Words,* 15.
68. Mother Teresa, *Total Surrender,* 150–151.
69. Egan and Egan, 67.
70. Kathryn Spink, *Mother Teresa: A Complete Authorized Biography* (San Francisco: HarperSanFrancisco, 1997), 5.
71. *Mother Teresa's Reaching Out in Love,* 19–20.
72. Mother Teresa, *In the Heart of the World: Thoughts, Stories, and Prayers,* ed. Angelo Scolozzi (Ann Arbor, MI: Servant, 1995), Kindle edition, L-350.
73. United States Conference of Catholic Bishops, "When I Call for Help: A Pastoral Response to Domestic Violence Against Women" (Washington, DC: USCCB, 2002), http://www.usccb.org/issues-and-action/marriage-and-family/marriage/domestic-violence/when-i-call-for-help.cfm.
74. Mother Teresa, *No Greater Love,* 127.
75. For more information about Catholic post-abortive healing resources, visit the websites of Rachel's Vineyard (rachelsvineyard.org) and the Silent No More Awareness Campaign (www.silentnomoreawareness.org).
76. *Mother Teresa's Reaching Out in Love,* 28.

77. Wyatt North, *Mother Teresa: A Life Inspired* (Boston: Wyatt North, 2014), Kindle edition, 41.

78. Mother Teresa, *No Greater Love*, 151.

79. Mother Teresa, *Total Surrender,* 107.

80. John Vianney, "The Parish of Ars (J.V.)" in *Thoughts of the Curé of Ars* (n.p.: Ravenio, 2015), Kindle edition, L-217.

81. Mother Teresa, *Where There Is Love*, 4.

82. Mother Teresa, *No Greater Love*, 78.

83. *Mother Teresa's Reaching Out in Love,* 101.

84. Mother Teresa, *Thirsting for God*, 38.

85. See Matthew 26:6–13, Mark 14:3–9, and Luke 7:36–38.

86. "Does not nature itself teach you that if a man wears long hair, it is degrading to him, but if a woman has long hair, it is her glory?" (1 Corinthians 11:14–15).

87. Mother Teresa, *A Simple Path*, 153.

88. Mother Teresa, *Thirsting for God*, 18.

89. See Matthew 26:48–50.

90. Mother Teresa, *Where There Is Love*, 48.

91. Malcolm Muggeridge, *Something Beautiful for God* (San Francisco: Harper & Row, 1971), 125.

92. Mother Teresa, *Thirsting for God*, 12.

93. Mother Teresa, *Total Surrender,* 22.

94. Mother Teresa, *Where There Is Love*, 37.

95. Mother Teresa, *In the Heart of the World*, L-142.

96. "The Burial" on the website of Sanctuary Holy Sepulchre, Gerusalemme San Salvatore Convento Francescano, accessed May 14, 2016, http://www.sepulchre.custodia.org/default.asp?id=4144.

97. Mother Teresa, *One Heart Full of Love*, 15.

98. Mother Teresa, *No Greater Love*, 158.

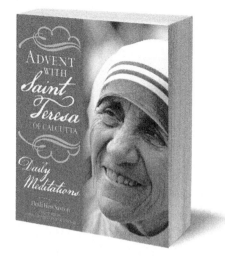

Take your own small steps in the footprints of this spiritual giant
through these Advent reflections based on the lectionary.
Each day features a meditation from Scripture
and a lesson from the life of St. Teresa.
Learn how this great saint can be your spiritual companion.

For other great Servant books on the life
and legacy of St. Teresa of Calcutta,
please go to shop.FranciscanMedia.org
or your local bookstore.

About the Author

Heidi Hess Saxton is a Catholic editor, wife, and mother, and author of several books. A convert to the Catholic faith since 1995, Saxton holds a master's in theology from Sacred Heart Major Seminary in Detroit. As part of her undergraduate studies at Bethany College of Missions in Minneapolis, she spent an internship in Senegal that sparked a lifelong interest in missions—an interest that connected her in a very personal way with the life and work of St. Teresa of Calcutta. Heidi is now editorial director of Servant, an imprint of Franciscan Media. She writes for adoptive, foster, and special-needs families at her blog, A Mother on the Road Less Traveled.